SASE Expl

A beginner's reterence
guide to Secure Access
Service Edge

For Arthur and Rufus
Always be curious.

Chapter 1: Welcome to the Wonderful World of SASE

Hello there and thank you for picking up this book! Whether you are a seasoned Networking Pro, a super-secret Security spy, or someone just starting to explore the realm of SASE; there will be some content waiting in these pages for you.

Now, I am not going to start this book with a lie. At the heart of it, SASE is not new. Gartner defined the term back in 2019, but even then, it was focused on taking all the good stuff from networking, and all the difficult stuff of Security, and merging them into a single platform. A converged platform some may say! This dramatically improved the lives of people who adopted SASE, as the traditional approach of 'silos' within an organization were rapidly broken down. IT Engineers working together with Security analysts? Preposterous (I hear you say), well that used to be the case before SASE came along.

Now as time marched on from 2019, new pieces of technology and new components have been added to the SASE mix, and this will continue to evolve. This is where the exciting aspect of SASE starts to manifest. SASE is not a product; it is not something you can 'achieve', and it is not something that can be completed. It's a shifting framework that constantly changes, and requires changing, just like the cybersecurity world we are all familiar with (or scared of!)

So, what is it about SASE that compelled me to author this book?

Look around you. How many pieces of technology do you still use where you must actively consult a manual? For your dishwasher, fridge, phone, television, and any other user good, the answer is never. But these are items that we rely on every day, and in some cases, are seen as an inseparable part of our lives. So why is it that we take this approach with the 'low stakes' items, however we leave our organizational connectivity, and security, to tools that are so incredibly complex (and disjointed) that there's confusion to even those who dedicate their life to studying these items?

The more tools you use, the greater the complexity of the solution. The more points of connectivity, the greater the chance of gaps, stress fractures or incompatible integrations between each of the tools. This is where the threat actor jumps in and uses chaos and confusion to steal all your data. SASE helps prevent this by unifying, simplifying, and connecting all your stuff together to help mitigate this pain.

Secure, protect connect. It is a mantra I live by.

Now, when talking with many industry CIOs/CTOs, there's often confusion about what SASE really means. Each vendor has their own interpretation and approach, some play to their strengths, while others besmirch the competition to hide their limitations. We will not be doing that here, this book is vendor agnostic, honestly – I do not really care which vendor you use. The important thing is that you find a way to ensure that all edges of your environment to keep the important stuff secure, and the data flowing in the right direction.

Now will you learn absolutely everything you need to know about SASE in this book? I doubt it. The market landscape is expanding quicker than I can type, however will you have a better understanding of the concepts and components that make up SASE? Well, I hope so.

Also, do not read this cover to cover in a single sitting. You will not remember it, and you will feel bored. Now, on with the next chapter we head!

Chapter 2: The Evolution of Enterprise Networks

Imagine a bustling city. Cars zoom along highways, pedestrians' stride along sidewalks, and the hum of activity is constant. This city is your business, and each vehicle or pedestrian represents a packet of data traveling across your network. In the past, the infrastructure of this 'city' was relatively simple. Data packets traveled predictable routes, and the traffic was easy to manage. However, as technology has advanced, so too have the demands placed on our data highways. Welcome to the story of the evolution of enterprise networks!

In the early days of networking - let's call it the 'Small Town Era' - things were simple. A company's network was a self-contained entity. Everything revolved around the data center, the 'town center' if you will. Traffic was predictable, and security was as simple as a 'city wall' - a firewall that kept the good stuff in and the bad stuff out. This model, known as the hub-and-spoke network, was like the structure of a small town where everything happens in the center and people commute in and out.

But then, along came the 'Suburban Boom'. As businesses grew and expanded, so did their networks. Branch offices started popping up, just like suburban neighborhoods. Employees were no longer confined to a single location, and data packets started commuting longer distances. Wide Area Networks (WANs) came into being to connect these spread-out entities. It was the beginning of the networking revolution.

But the suburban boom wasn't without its challenges. Picture traffic congestion at rush hour. Just as more cars on the road mean more traffic jams, more data flowing across a network meant slower speeds and higher latency. The once peaceful small town was now a sprawling city with traffic problems. Enter the era of the 'Metropolis'. Cloud computing and Software-as-a-Service (SaaS) applications added even more complexity to the mix. Now, data wasn't just traveling between offices, but also to and from the cloud. The traditional model of routing all traffic through the data center was like having all city traffic funneled through a single intersection – a recipe for gridlock.

And then there was the 'security suburbs' problem. In the old small-town model, security was straightforward. But as the network city expanded, securing all the suburbs became a challenge. The traditional city wall or firewall was no longer enough.

This brings us to the current era - the 'Global Village'. With the advent of the Internet of Things (IoT), mobile devices, and remote work, the network city has become a global village. Data packets now travel not just between offices and the cloud, but also to and from homes, coffee shops, and even across continents. The old hub-and-spoke model? It's as outdated as a horse-drawn carriage in a city of self-driving cars.

So, what's the answer to the challenges of the global village? Welcome to the world of Secure Access Service Edge (SASE), where the city planning of networking takes a novel and exciting turn. But we're getting ahead of ourselves. That's a thrilling journey we'll embark on in the upcoming chapters.

The evolution of enterprise networks from small towns to global villages is a tale of innovation, adaptation, and the relentless march of technology. But it's also a story of challenges - traffic congestion, security threats, and managing a complex, global infrastructure. As we turn the page, we will delve deeper into how SASE addresses these challenges, transforming the bustling, often chaotic global village into a harmonious, secure, and highly efficient smart city.

As we stand on the precipice of this 'Global Village' era, it's worth taking a moment to look back at the road we've traveled. In our city analogy, we've witnessed the evolution from a one-stoplight town to a bustling metropolis. Now, as we face the demands of this global village, we must understand that our old way of managing traffic simply won't work.

Just like how a city evolves and adapts to the needs of its residents, so too must our network evolve to meet the demands of our data traffic. But what does that look like? Imagine a city where the roads are smart, able to redirect traffic based on real-time conditions. A city where security is integrated into the very fabric of its infrastructure, seamlessly protecting its inhabitants. This is the vision of SASE, and it's the destination we're heading towards on this journey.

Before we get there, though, let's revisit some of the pain points that have emerged along the way. We've already discussed the traffic jams that came with the 'Suburban Boom' and the 'Metropolis' era. But consider also the wear and tear on our infrastructure. Just as city roads can develop potholes and cracks, so too can our networks start to strain under the weight of ever-increasing traffic. The patchwork repairs we've applied in the past - adding more bandwidth, deploying additional hardware - are temporary fixes at best.

And then there's the issue of security. In the 'Small Town' era, it was easy to see who was coming and going. But as our network city has grown, keeping track of all the data packets traveling across our networks has become an increasingly complex task. It's like trying to monitor every car, bike, and pedestrian in a bustling metropolis - a near-impossible task with our current tools.

Finally, there's the challenge of visibility and control. As our networks have expanded, keeping an eye on all the moving parts has become harder and harder. Imagine being the mayor of a city and not knowing what's happening in your suburbs, let alone in the remote neighborhoods. It's a daunting task, and one that's all too familiar to network administrators in this era of the global village.

So, how does SASE fit into this picture? To stick with our city analogy, imagine SASE as the ultimate city planner. It's a framework that brings together networking and security into a single, unified model. Instead of separate systems for traffic management and security, SASE integrates these functions into a cohesive whole.

SASE also embraces the principles of the 'smart city'. It leverages cloud computing and artificial intelligence to manage traffic more efficiently and secure the network more effectively. It's like having self-driving cars that can avoid traffic jams and identify potential threats - all managed by a sophisticated AI system that keeps the city running smoothly.

As we delve deeper into SASE in the upcoming chapters, we'll explore how this innovative approach can help us navigate the challenges of our network city. We'll look at how it can streamline traffic, enhance security, and provide better visibility and control. But for now, let's revel in the journey we've taken so far. From the small town to the global village, it's been a wild ride - and the best is yet to come!

Chapter 3: Understanding the SASE Framework

The Grand Blueprint

Think back to the biggest puzzle you've ever completed. Hundreds, maybe even thousands of pieces, each unique but all necessary to create the full picture. The Secure Access Service Edge (SASE) framework is somewhat like that grand puzzle, a collection of several components, each playing a crucial role to form a comprehensive, secure, and efficient network.

In the previous chapter, we saw our network city evolve from a small town to a sprawling global village. Now, it's time to consider our city's blueprint - a plan that ensures efficient traffic management, robust security, and seamless connectivity for all. That's what the SASE framework offers. It's the grand design that brings together the best of networking and security in a cloud-centric model.

Components of SASE: The Puzzle Pieces

As we delve into the heart of SASE, it's crucial to understand its core components. These are the building blocks - or, to continue our analogy, the puzzle pieces - that make up our SASE city. Let's start with the first one: the convergence of networking and security.

Convergence of Networking and Security

In our network city, we've always had separate systems for managing traffic (networking) and security. It's like having one team responsible for traffic lights and another for city security. But what if we could integrate these two functions? That's the basic idea behind SASE's convergence of networking and security. It's like having a smart traffic light that not only manages traffic flow but also identifies potential threats.

Cloud-Native Architecture

In our evolving city, we've seen how crucial the cloud has become. With SASE, the cloud isn't just another suburb; it's the very foundation of our city's architecture. SASE is cloud-native, meaning it's designed to fully leverage the scalability, flexibility, and accessibility of the cloud. It's like moving from a traditional city layout to a futuristic, high-tech city where everything is interconnected and easily adjustable.

Identity-Driven Access

In our global village, knowing who's who and who gets to go where is paramount. That's why SASE uses identity-driven access. This approach considers the identity of a user or device before deciding what network resources it can access. It's like having a smart ID card that automatically grants you access to the buildings and services you're authorized to use.

The Puzzle Comes Together: SASE in Action

With a deeper understanding of these core SASE components, we can start to see the grand picture. The puzzle pieces come together to form a network architecture that is not only more secure and efficient but also more adaptable and responsive to the ever-changing demands of our global village.

The convergence of networking and security creates a holistic system where traffic management and security enforcement go hand in hand. The cloud-native architecture ensures that our network city can scale and adapt with the agility of a high-tech metropolis. Identity-driven access ensures that every resident of our city - be they user, device, or application - has appropriate access rights, enhancing both security and efficiency.

In the next section, we'll delve deeper into how SASE revolutionizes network and security management, transforming our network city into a highly secure, efficient, and adaptable smart city. So, buckle up, fellow travelers, our tour of the SASE city is just getting started!

Chapter 4: The Revolution in Network Management: SASE in Action

---

An Architectural Uprising

Welcome back, fellow city explorers! As we dive into Chapter 4, we're taking a hard hat tour of our SASE city's construction site. Here, we'll see the impact of the SASE framework in revolutionizing network management. This is where the rubber meets the road, where we move from theory into practice. Buckle up, it's time to see SASE in action!

Unifying the Command Center

We start our journey at the city's command center. Remember the days when we had separate teams managing different aspects of our city – traffic control, security, public services? Well, those days are behind us in our SASE city. Instead, we have a unified command center where everything is controlled from one place. It's the nerve center of our city, a bustling hub of activity that oversees everything from traffic flow to security.

In practical terms, this means networking and security services are consolidated into a single, cloud-based platform. Imagine all your network traffic flowing through one system that simultaneously optimizes connectivity and enforces security policies. It's a holistic approach that eliminates the inefficiencies and blind spots that can occur when these services are managed separately.

Evolving Traffic Patterns

Next, let's take a look at how traffic moves around our SASE city. Unlike traditional network architectures that follow a predictable, rigid path, traffic in a SASE network is dynamic and adaptable. This fluidity is akin to a smart traffic system that can adjust routes in real-time based on traffic volume, road conditions, and even the destination of each vehicle.

In a SASE architecture, network traffic is routed based on factors such as the identity of the user or device, the sensitivity of the data being accessed, and current network conditions. This dynamic, policy-driven approach ensures that network resources are used efficiently, and that sensitive data always travels along the most secure path.

Advanced Security Patrol

Security in our SASE city isn't just about keeping the bad guys out. It's also about ensuring that every user and device behaves appropriately while they're inside the city. This is achieved through advanced security services such as Secure Web Gateways (SWG), Firewall-as-a-Service (FWaaS), and Zero Trust Network Access (ZTNA).

Think of these services as our city's security patrol, constantly monitoring the city, ensuring everyone follows the rules, and ready to spring into action at the first sign of trouble. With these advanced security services, threats can be detected and neutralized more quickly, and potentially harmful behavior can be stopped before it leads to serious consequences.

The Dawn of the SASE Era

As we witness the construction of our SASE city, it's clear that we're not just building another network architecture. We're forging a new era in network management, an era defined by the convergence of networking and security, the flexible and scalable nature of cloud-native architecture, and the precision of identity-driven access.

As we move forward on this journey, we'll explore more about how SASE can be implemented, the challenges that may arise, and how to overcome them. But for now, let's take a moment to appreciate the revolutionary nature of what we're building. In our SASE city, network management isn't just about maintaining the status quo; it's about constantly striving for a better, more efficient, and more secure way of doing things. It's about breaking down the barriers between networking and security and creating a unified, holistic system.

And as we stand here at the construction site of our SASE city, we can already see the first rays of dawn breaking over the horizon, heralding the start of a new day, a new era in network management. The SASE era.

Cloud-native architecture enables resources to be provisioned and de-provisioned on-demand, flexibly adjusting to the ebb and flow of network demand. Need to connect a new branch office? No problem. Experiencing a sudden surge in remote workers? SASE can handle it. It's as if our city can instantly add new roads, bridges, or buses whenever needed, always ensuring smooth traffic flow.

Redefining Network Perimeters

Traditionally, network security has been focused on protecting the network perimeter - the boundary between the 'trusted' internal network and the 'untrusted' external network. But in our global village, this boundary has become increasingly blurred. Remote work, mobile devices, and cloud services have all extended the network perimeter, making it harder to secure.

SASE addresses this challenge by redefining the concept of the network perimeter. Instead of a fixed boundary, SASE treats every access point - whether it's a remote worker, a mobile device, or a cloud service - as a dynamic, individual perimeter. Each of these perimeters is secured based on the user's or device's identity and the sensitivity of the data being accessed.

Imagine a city where every building, park, and home has its own secure perimeter, adjusted based on who's accessing it and why. That's the level of granularity and control that SASE brings to network security.

As we conclude this chapter, we see the power of SASE in revolutionizing network management. Its convergence of networking and security, cloud-native architecture, identity-driven access, and use of AI all come together to create a network that is not only secure and efficient, but also flexible and scalable. In the next chapter, we'll be stepping into the future of our city and the incredible possibilities that the SASE framework opens. But for now, let's marvel at the architectural wonder that is our SASE city - a testament to the power of innovation and progress.

Chapter 5: Meeting the Future: The Incredible Possibilities of SASE

The Ever-Evolving Cityscape

Welcome back, fellow explorers of the SASE city! As we forge ahead into Chapter 5, we're stepping into a time machine and fast-forwarding to the future. What will our city look like when SASE is fully implemented? Let's gaze into the crystal ball and explore the incredible possibilities of SASE.

Towards A User-Centric Approach

The first significant change we'll see is a shift towards a user-centric approach. With SASE, network resources are no longer confined to a specific location; instead, they can be accessed by users wherever they are. It's like turning our city into a global village, where services aren't just available in specific buildings but can be accessed anywhere, anytime.

This approach ensures that whether a user is in the head office, a branch office, or working remotely, they'll enjoy the same level of network performance and security. It's a game-changer for organizations with a distributed workforce, making it easier than ever to work from anywhere.

The Rise of the Intelligent Network

With the implementation of SASE, our city won't just be connected; it'll be intelligent. Thanks to AI and machine learning, SASE networks can analyze traffic patterns, predict network issues, and respond to security threats in real time.

This intelligence allows the network to self-optimize, dynamically adjusting its operation based on current conditions. It's like having a smart city management system that can predict traffic jams before they happen, optimize power usage based on demand, and even detect potential infrastructure issues before they cause problems.

Enhanced Security: Protection from Every Angle

In the future SASE city, security will be more robust than ever. With the convergence of networking and security, every data packet moving through the network will be inspected and secured. Coupled with advanced security services such as SWG, FWaaS, and ZTNA, this ensures a high level of protection from a wide range of threats.

Plus, with SASE's identity-driven access, the network will be able to enforce granular access control, ensuring that users and devices only have access to the resources they need. It's like having a smart security system that not only keeps out intruders but also ensures that residents only access areas they're authorized to enter.

Adapting to Change: The Agility of SASE

One of the greatest strengths of SASE is its agility. Thanks to its cloud-native design, a SASE network can easily scale up or down as needed. This flexibility allows it to easily adapt to changes, whether it's a sudden surge in network demand, the addition of a new branch office, or a shift in work patterns.

In our future SASE city, this agility will ensure that the network can keep up with the pace of change, always ready to adapt to whatever the future holds.

Seamless Integration with the Internet of Things (IoT)

As we gaze into the future of our SASE city, we can't ignore the role of the Internet of Things (IoT). More and more devices are coming online each day - from home appliances and wearables to industrial sensors and smart city infrastructure. Each of these connected devices becomes a resident in our SASE city, necessitating efficient management and rigorous security.

SASE's identity-driven approach makes it ideally suited to manage IoT devices. Just like how residents of a city have specific access rights, each IoT device will be given access based on its role and the data it handles. A temperature sensor in a factory, for example, doesn't need access to financial records - and with SASE, it won't have it.

Promoting Sustainability through Efficient Resource Usage

In our future SASE city, sustainability is key. The cloud-native nature of SASE allows for efficient use of resources, reducing waste and promoting sustainability. Traditional network infrastructures often require substantial hardware, leading to significant energy consumption and electronic waste. By moving the bulk of network operations to the cloud, SASE significantly reduces these environmental impacts.

Enabling Digital Transformation

SASE isn't just a new network architecture; it's a catalyst for digital transformation. By simplifying network management and enhancing security, SASE removes many of the obstacles that organizations face when embarking on digital transformation initiatives.

Whether it's moving to cloud-based services, adopting AI and machine learning, or enabling remote work, digital transformation often relies on a robust, secure, and flexible network. With its cloud-centric design and integrated security, SASE provides the ideal foundation for these transformative initiatives.

Fostering Innovation and Collaboration

Lastly, SASE isn't just about the nuts and bolts of network architecture; it's about the people who use the network. By delivering a seamless and secure user experience, SASE can help foster innovation and collaboration.

Imagine a team of developers scattered across the globe, collaborating on a new software product. Or a team of scientists sharing large datasets for a climate research project. In both cases, SASE's ability to provide secure, high-performance connectivity regardless of location or device can empower these teams to collaborate more effectively, driving innovation and progress.

A Bright Future Ahead

The future SASE city looks promising indeed. With its seamless integration with IoT, commitment to sustainability, role in enabling digital transformation, and potential to foster innovation and collaboration, SASE promises a bright future for network management.

As we continue our journey through this book, we'll begin to explore the steps needed to build our future SASE city. From planning and implementation to troubleshooting and maintenance, we'll guide you through the process of turning the promise of SASE into reality. But for now, let's take a moment to celebrate the potential of this transformative approach, and look forward to the incredible possibilities that lie ahead.

Chapter 6: The Evolution of Digital Transformation and the Role of SASE

Digital Transformation: A Journey through Time

As we've journeyed through the previous chapters, we've seen glimpses of the profound impact of SASE on the city of the future. In Chapter 6, we step back from the architecture of our city to examine the broader context in which it exists. We're zooming out to view the city from above, amidst the sweeping currents of digital transformation that have reshaped the business landscape.

Digital transformation is not a recent phenomenon, but rather an evolutionary process that's been occurring for decades. To understand its full impact and the role of SASE within it, we need to embark on a trip through time, observing how businesses have adopted technology to drive change, innovation, and growth.

The origins of digital transformation can be traced back to the advent of digital computers in the 1950s and 1960s. Businesses started using these machines to automate simple tasks, such as data storage and calculations, leading to the first wave of digital transformation. This era was characterized by the digitization of manual tasks and the creation of digital databases.

Fast forward to the 1990s, and the invention of the internet marked the next significant phase of digital transformation. Businesses started to realize the potential of this new medium, leading to the birth of e-commerce. This period saw the digital transformation move beyond just internal processes to encompass customer-facing functions, revolutionizing the way businesses interacted with their customers.

The 2000s heralded the age of cloud computing, taking digital transformation to new heights. The cloud allowed businesses to store data and run applications in centralized data centers, accessed over the internet.

This shift enabled organizations to operate more efficiently, scale rapidly, and innovate quicker. Businesses were no longer constrained by their own physical infrastructure and could leverage the power of the cloud to drive growth and transformation.

In the 2010s, two significant trends shaped digital transformation: mobility and big data. The explosion of smartphones and tablets redefined how businesses interacted with customers and employees, leading to the creation of mobile apps and the rise of remote work. Meanwhile, the advent of big data - the ability to capture, store, and analyze vast amounts of data - allowed businesses to gain unprecedented insights into their operations and customer behaviors.

Today, digital transformation is an integral part of almost every business strategy. Technologies such as AI, machine learning, IoT, and blockchain are driving further innovation and transformation. Businesses are not only digitizing their operations but also fundamentally rethinking their business models, products, and services. We are in an era where digital technology is not just supporting the business; it is the business.

So, where does SASE fit into this historical tableau? As we've discussed, SASE is a convergence of network and security services into a single, cloud-native service model. It reflects the current trends of digital transformation, from cloud adoption and mobility to AI and machine learning.

Just as cities need a robust infrastructure to support growth and change, businesses undergoing digital transformation need a strong network foundation. That's where SASE comes in. By providing a scalable, secure, and efficient network architecture, SASE enables businesses to embrace digital transformation with confidence.

The adoption of SASE goes together with the modern approach to digital transformation. As businesses increasingly adopt cloud services, support remote work, and leverage big data and AI, they need a network architecture that can support these initiatives. By offering a unified, cloud-native platform, SASE allows businesses to seamlessly integrate their network and security operations, facilitating their digital transformation journey.

The Digital-First World and SASE

Today, we live in a digital-first world, where technology is no longer an add-on but a necessity. Companies have shifted from traditional business models to more digital ones, like the shift from brick-

and-mortar stores to e-commerce platforms, or from traditional cable to streaming services. This has opened the door to new opportunities, but also new challenges. SASE, with its integration of networking and security, is primed to support these new business models and tackle the challenges they present.

For example, consider an e-commerce company with a global customer base. This company needs a robust network to ensure its website is accessible and performs well for customers around the world. At the same time, it needs a robust security system to protect sensitive customer data. SASE provides a unified solution, delivering high network performance and security from a single, cloud-native platform.

SASE and the Distributed Workforce

Digital transformation also includes changes in the workplace. We're seeing a shift towards a distributed workforce, with employees working from different locations and even different time zones. This trend was accelerated by the COVID-19 pandemic, which forced companies to adopt remote work practically overnight.

With a distributed workforce, the traditional network perimeter no longer exists. Instead, security must be enforced at the level of individual users and devices, no matter where they are. This is precisely what SASE does. It treats each access point as a dynamic perimeter, securing it based on the identity of the user or device and the sensitivity of the data being accessed.

Digital Transformation and the Future of SASE

Looking towards the future, as digital transformation continues to evolve, so will the role of SASE. Technologies like 5G and edge computing will create new opportunities for businesses, but also new network and security challenges. As these technologies come into play, SASE's ability to provide flexible, scalable, and secure connectivity will be more crucial than ever.

Moreover, as companies increasingly rely on data to drive their operations and decision-making, the need for a secure and efficient network infrastructure will only grow. SASE, with its ability to secure data in transit and optimize network performance, will play a key role in enabling businesses to harness the power of data.

SASE: A Catalyst for Digital Transformation

In conclusion, SASE is not just a response to digital transformation; it's a catalyst for it. By providing a unified, cloud-native network and security platform, SASE enables businesses to embrace digital transformation with greater confidence and less complexity.

Whether it's supporting new digital business models, enabling a distributed workforce, or preparing for future technologies, SASE provides the network backbone that modern businesses need. In the next chapters, we'll explore how you can implement SASE in your organization and take your digital transformation journey to the next level.

Chapter 7: Let's Get Technical. What is SD-WAN?

Software-Defined WAN

Software-Defined Wide-Area-Network (SD-WAN) is defined as a virtual WAN architecture that allows enterprises to securely and efficiently connect users to applications. This technology solution brings unparalleled agility and cost savings to networking. With SD-WAN, organizations can deliver more responsive, more predictable applications at a lower cost in less time than the managed MPLS services traditionally used by the enterprise. IT becomes far more agile, deploying sites in minutes; leveraging any available data service such as MPLS, dedicated Internet access (DIA), broadband, or wireless; and being able to reconfigure sites instantly.

SD-WAN does this by separating applications from the underlying network services with a policy-based, virtual overlay. This overlay monitors the real-time performance characteristics of the underlying networks and selects the optimum network for each application based on configuration policies.

What is SD-WAN Technology?

SD-WAN technology is a new way to manage and optimize a wide area network. It is designed to address the changing use of enterprise networks due to the growth of cloud computing and mobile devices. It is a more flexible solution than MPLS, better supports a distributed and mobile workforce, and is more reliable and scalable than VPN-based WAN.

SD-WAN is implemented as a network of SD-WAN appliances connected by encrypted tunnels. Each SD-WAN appliance is connected to a set of network services (typically MPLS and some Internet services) and monitors the current availability and performance of each of these services. Traffic reaching an SD-WAN appliance is classified based upon application and prioritized using a set of centrally-managed priorities before being sent out over the best available network link.

SD-WAN makes it possible to replace MPLS, which is expensive and time-consuming to connect to new locations. It also allows security functionality to be distributed to the network edge, making it unnecessary to send all traffic through the enterprise data center for scanning before forwarding it to cloud services, a practice that degrades latency and performance. By converging networking and security functionality, an SD-WAN can eliminate the need to deploy expensive point security products at branch locations. An SD-WAN with a large network of globally-distributed points-of-presence (PoPs) can provide high-performance, secure networking with centralized management and visibility.

A History of SD-WAN

Software-defined WAN (SD-WAN) brings the abstraction of SDN to the WAN; however, it is only the latest in a series of transformations of WAN.

The very first stage of WAN, in the 1980s, used point-to-point (PPP) lines to connect different LANs. The price and efficiency of these connections were improved with the introduction of Frame Relay in the early 1990s. Instead of requiring a direct PPP connection between each pair of communicating parties, Frame Relay allowed connection to a "cloud" from a service provider, allowing shared last-mile link bandwidth and the use of less expensive router hardware.

The next stage was the introduction of Multiprotocol Label Switching (MPLS), which provided an IP-based means of carrying voice, video, and data on the same network. MPLS provides dependable network connections protected by SLAs but is expensive and slow to provision.

In 2013, SD-WAN emerged, showing the potential to be a viable and cost-effective alternative to MPLS – making it the logical next step in WAN technology. By abstracting away the network layer and routing traffic based upon a collection of centrally defined and managed policies, SD-WAN is able to optimize routing and prioritization of various types of application traffic. The flexibility provided by SD-WAN also allows it to better meet the needs of cloud and mobile users. As this type of use is becoming more common, it is unsurprising that many organizations are anticipated to adopt SD-WAN.

SD-WAN 1.0 - Hungry for Bandwidth

The first stage of SD-WAN evolution was focused on solving the issues of availability and last-mile bandwidth. New MPLS links are expensive and slow to provision, and the use of an Internet backup meant that the backup was only used in the case of an outage.

The predecessor to SD-WAN provided some improvements with link-bonding, which combines multiple Internet services with diverse technologies, such as xDSL and 4G from different providers. This technology operated at the link layer and improved last-mile bandwidth. These improvements were limited to the last mile and did not create benefits for the middle mile. Although the network was not yet virtualized at this stage, the idea was laying the groundwork for SD-WAN and proving to be a solution to the changing needs of enterprise networks.

SD-WAN 2.0 - The Rise of SD-WAN startups

Link bonding only addressed the availability of the last mile. For true improvement in WAN performance, routing awareness needs to take place anywhere along the path, not just the last mile. Advanced features beyond link bonding were needed to address current needs. As these new advancements in SD-WAN were being developed, many startups soon appeared on the scene. Competition breeds innovation, and this phase introduced new features such as virtualization failover/failback capabilities and application-aware routing. These features were driven by the need for improved performance and agility on the WAN. SD-WAN improves the agility of the WAN by avoiding the installation and provisioning delays of MPLS and fills the need for bandwidth on demand. Virtualization allows network administrators the ability to manage the paths or the services underneath from a single control panel to configure optimization features.

Optimization of SD-WAN provides application performance that previously required the SLA-backed connections of MPLS. Using application-aware routing and dynamic link assessment, SD-WAN improves WAN performance by selecting the optimum connection per application. SD-WAN met the challenge to deliver the right performance and uptime characteristics needed to provide applications to users.

SD-WAN 3.0 – Reaching Out

SD-WAN evolved beyond connecting branch offices — expanding the reach to all enterprise resources to create a seamless network experience. This is a major shift in networking capabilities to create a unified infrastructure for cloud, mobility, and "as-a-service" technologies. SD-WAN provides encrypted Internet tunnels for traffic traversing the WAN. SD-WAN as-a-service can provide a full enterprise-grade, network security stack built directly into its global SD-WAN backbone to protect all location types, including mobile users.

What's the Difference between SD-WAN and SDN?

SD-WANs implement software-defined networking (SDN) principles to connect locations. SDNs first were introduced in the data center with the goal of increasing the network by separating the data plane from the control plane. The policies and routing intelligence would run in one or more servers ("controllers"), which would instruct the networking elements forwarding the packets (switches and routers).

SDN created an overlay across the local network, opening up a world of possibilities in efficiency and agility. SD-WAN creates an overlay across the wide-area network also bringing incredible efficiency and agility gains.

Why Do Enterprises Need SD-WAN?

The cloud and high levels of mobility characterize how people use networks today. WANs, however, were designed in an era in which the focus was on linking physical locations. Using the old approach to support the new needs results in expensive global connectivity, complex topologies, and widely dispersed "point products" that are difficult to maintain and secure.

The unending and cumbersome cycle of patching, updating, and upgrading requires skilled techs, an increasingly scarce commodity. That's especially distressing because all this complexity is an inviting target for hackers, who can exploit misconfigurations, software vulnerabilities, and other attack surfaces.

There are several reasons that legacy WANs no longer are up to the job. MPLS, the focal point of the old approach, is expensive and requires long lead times for deployment to new locations. Legacy WANs only touch the Internet at secure Web portals, usually at the data center. This leads to the "trombone" effect of sending Web data back and forth across networks. The result is added latency and exhaustion of the supply of MPLS links as Internet traffic increases. Direct Internet access, which would link branch offices to the Internet, is expensive and could overwhelm rudimentary branch hardware. Finally, the WAN was designed when the emphasis was on linking physical assets such as offices and data centers. This approach isn't ideal for this new and varied world.

Though SD-WAN brings many benefits, there are also key limitations. Extending the SD-WAN to the cloud requires installing an SD-WAN in or near the cloud provider's data center, a complicated if not impossible task. Mobile users are entirely ignored by SD-WAN.

And while traffic is encrypted, exposing branches to the Internet raises the threat of malware, phishing emails, and other attacks. Deploying security appliances at the branch means that continuing with the costs of purchasing, sizing, and maintenance associated with security appliances continues. Enterprises are still forced into upgrading appliances, and IT needs to apply the full range of security functions, as traffic volumes grow. Finally, troubleshooting is also made more difficult as personnel has to jump between networking and security consoles to reach the root cause. This is inefficient and can lead to errors and overlooked information about the problem at hand.

The emerging option is to converge security and networking functions together into cloud-scale software. All Internet and WAN traffic is sent to and received from the provider's point of presence (PoP) running the software. PoPs, in turn, communicate over their own backbone, avoiding the performance problems associated with the Internet core. This approach is known as SD-WAN as a service or SD-WAN 3.0.

The important point is that the challenges of running both networking and security stacks at the branch office are alleviated. The SD-WAN devices in this case form from a "thin edge" with minimal processing. The main task that these devices perform is to assess packets to determine whether they should be sent to the Internet, to the MPLS links, or elsewhere. With the core security and networking process done in the cloud, SD-WAN as a service can continue to inspect traffic at line rate regardless of the traffic volumes or enabled features.

An SD-WAN managed service is a carrier- or service provider-based SD-WAN offering. It guarantees the organization a certain level of performance across its network. The carrier provides the transport and connects the enterprise to real and virtual technology at the carrier data center and perhaps in third-party clouds.

SD-WAN managed services don't answer the question of how to secure branch-based Internet access. They are simply different business and management approaches to the same technological infrastructure.

How does SD-WAN Work?

Software-defined WAN (SD-WAN) is designed to solve many of the challenges associated with traditional WAN design. SD-WAN abstracts away the details of the networking layer, allowing the WAN to use a variety of different connection types interchangeably, including LTE, MPLS, and broadband Internet. This abstraction can improve network bandwidth, performance, and redundancy and enables centralized management and orchestration.

SD-WAN works by creating a network of SD-WAN appliances connected by encrypted tunnels. Each site on the WAN has its own SD-WAN appliance, and all traffic flows through that appliance. Since all appliances are centrally managed, consistent networking policies can be enforced throughout the organization. When traffic enters an SD-WAN appliance, the appliance determines the type of application traffic and routes it to its destination based upon existing policies and the availability and performance of different network links.

Traditional SD-WAN is hardly perfect. Many SD-WANs do not include integrated security, so each branch location must deploy its own standalone security products. SD-WAN also includes the deployment of an SD-WAN appliance at each endpoint, which makes it difficult or impossible to use it for cloud and mobile traffic. Finally, SD-WAN often relies upon the public Internet, which can cause reliability concerns. However, many of these problems are solved with secure access service edge (SASE) platforms.

SD-WAN Security

MPLS and appliance-based software-defined WAN (SD-WAN) can both provide an organization with the networking capabilities needed for a WAN. However, they often have significant security shortcomings. MPLS lacks any encryption of its circuits, and both MPLS and appliance-based SD-WAN may have no built-in security. As a result, many organizations using these systems deploy standalone security appliances at each location to provide the necessary cybersecurity protections.

However, this approach to WAN security can be complex, unscalable, and expensive since each new location requires another set of security appliances. Each of these appliances must be individually purchased, configured, monitored, and managed, which creates significant costs throughout their lifetimes. This approach also does not work for the cloud and mobile, where security appliances cannot be deployed on-site.

Cloud-based SD-WAN provides a solution to this problem. By placing points-of-presence (PoPs) in the cloud, they can achieve global coverage, allowing users to connect via a nearby PoP and use the SD-WAN with minimal latency impacts. These PoPs can also have integrated security functionality, removing the need to deploy standalone appliances at each location and enabling centralized networking and security visibility across the enterprise WAN. Networking and security integration can also improve performance since networking and security appliances can be optimized to interoperate with one another.

Designed to provide an alternative to traditional MPLS-based WAN, Software-defined WAN (SD-WAN) provides organizations with five major benefits when compared to MPLS.

1. Reduced WAN Costs - MPLS bandwidth is expensive, and it can take weeks or months to provision a new MPLS link, compared to days with SD-WAN. Both in cost of operation and in the lost business opportunity, MPLS is inferior to SD-WAN.

2. Enhanced WAN performance - MPLS is very effective at routing traffic between two static locations, but the growth of the cloud makes this less useful to businesses. SD-WAN's policy-based routing allows traffic to be optimally sent through the network based on the needs of the underlying application.

3. Improved WAN agility - SD-WAN also provides much more agile networking than MPLS. With SD-WAN, the network layer is abstracted away, allowing the use of a variety of different transport mechanisms throughout the WAN.

4. Simplified WAN management - With MPLS, an organization may need to deploy a variety of standalone appliances to manage WAN optimization and security. With SD-WAN, these operations can be centralized, allowing organizations to scalably manage growing networks.

5. Increased WAN availability - Finally, SD-WAN can provide dramatic redundancy and availability improvements over MPLS. With MPLS, adding redundant links can be expensive. SD-WAN, on the other hand, can route traffic over a different transport mechanism in the case of an outage.

SD-WAN Shortcomings

While SD-WAN technology brings many benefits, there are still some concerns if you solely leverage SD-WAN (and not SASE). These include:

1. SD-WAN is poorly suited for today's cloud- or mobile-centric enterprises. SD-WAN requires a device to be installed on each side of a connection but installing an SD-WAN device in or near a cloud provider's data center isn't trivial. And no SD-WAN

connects mobile users. All of this means that your many applications, data, and users will be poorly serviced or outright ignored by your SD-WAN. That's a mistake.

2. What's more SD-WAN lack integrated branch security. This presents an enormous challenge as branch offices all but requires direct, secure Internet access. Enterprises are forced to integrate and maintain third-party firewalls, IPSs, and SWGs, significantly complicating and increasing the costs of SD-WAN deployments.

3. Finally, most SD-WAN solutions rely on the public Internet, exposing enterprise traffic to the irregularities and unpredictability of Internet routing. This becomes particularly important in global routes where the combination of long delays and poor routing dramatically reduces throughput. And nor does SD-WAN alone have the necessary WAN optimization technologies to overcome the effects of high latency and packet loss that enterprises traditionally used to improve global connection throughput.

All these items must be considered when looking to choose a SASE or SD-WAN approach. I do not want to spoil things for you, but SASE is the way forward!

Chapter 7: Demystifying Zero Trust Network Access (ZTNA): Concepts, Ideas, and Implementation

The Birth of Zero Trust

Before we dive headlong into Zero Trust Network Access (ZTNA), it's worth understanding the philosophical underpinning that gave rise to it - the concept of Zero Trust. Born in the age of cloud and mobility, Zero Trust emerged as a radical departure from the traditional network security model, which relied on the idea of a trusted internal network and an untrusted external one.

Under the conventional model, once a user or device gained access to the internal network - often by simply being physically present within an organization's premises - they were typically granted broad access to resources. However, this approach left organizations vulnerable to insider threats and lateral movement attacks, where a compromised user or device could access sensitive resources within the network.

In stark contrast, Zero Trust operates under the principle "never trust, always verify." It assumes that any user or device, regardless of where it's connecting from, could potentially be compromised and therefore should not automatically be trusted. Instead, every access request is verified, authenticated, and securely logged before access is granted. In other words, Zero Trust flips the traditional model on its head, moving from an implicit trust model to an explicit verification model.

What is Zero Trust Network Access (ZTNA)?

Having taken our philosophical detour, let's get back on the road and talk about ZTNA. Zero Trust Network Access is the practical application of the Zero Trust philosophy to network access. ZTNA solutions provide secure access to specific network-based applications (rather than the entire network) based on user identity, context, and policy adherence. They effectively create a secure micro-perimeter around each application, further reducing the potential attack surface.

One of the key ideas behind ZTNA is that the network is always considered hostile. This mindset holds true regardless of whether a user is trying to access resources from within a supposedly secure corporate network, or from a coffee shop WiFi network halfway across the world. The primary focus shifts from securing network access to securing application access, which is a more fine-grained and arguably more meaningful control point.

The Benefits of ZTNA

Adopting a ZTNA model offers several key benefits. It reduces the attack surface by limiting users to accessing only the applications they need to perform their jobs, thereby mitigating the risk of lateral movement attacks. ZTNA also improves visibility and control over network traffic, as every access request is logged and can be analyzed for suspicious activity. Furthermore, by decoupling access policies from network topology, ZTNA simplifies policy management and enables more granular control over access rights.

In addition, ZTNA can offer a better user experience. Because access policies are centrally managed and dynamically enforced, users can seamlessly access their applications from any device, anywhere, without having to navigate through VPNs or jump hosts.

How Does ZTNA Work?

Now that we've understood the basic concept and benefits of ZTNA, let's delve a little deeper into how it actually works.

Authentication and Authorization

The first step in any ZTNA system is authenticating the user. This usually involves a multi-factor authentication process to ensure the user is who they claim to be. After the user is authenticated, the ZTNA system checks if they have the necessary permissions to access the requested application. This step is referred to as authorization.

Micro-segmentation

Micro-segmentation is a key component of ZTNA. It involves dividing the network into multiple isolated segments (or micro-perimeters) around each application. By doing this, ZTNA limits the potential damage if a user or device is compromised. Even if an attacker manages to penetrate one micro-perimeter,

they are still isolated from other segments of the
network.

Least Privilege Access

Another fundamental principle of ZTNA is least
privilege access, which means granting users only the
access they need to perform their jobs and nothing
more. This minimizes the risk of over-privileged users
who have access to sensitive resources they don't need.

Implementing ZTNA

Implementing ZTNA in an organization can be a
complex process, but it typically involves the following
steps:

1. Identify sensitive applications: The first
    step is to identify the applications that need
    to be protected. These might include
    customer databases, financial systems,
    human resource applications, and others.

2. Define access policies: For each
    application, define who should have access,
    under what conditions, and to what extent.
    These policies should be based on the
    principle of least privilege.

3. Deploy ZTNA solution: Choose a ZTNA solution that fits your organization's needs and deploy it. This may involve installing software on user devices and application servers, and setting up a policy engine to enforce access policies.

4. Monitor and adjust: Once the ZTNA solution is deployed, continuously monitor its effectiveness and adjust access policies as needed.

As we'll see in the next section, the move towards ZTNA is very much aligned with the broader transition towards SASE. Let's explore this connection further.

ZTNA and SASE: A Perfect Match

As we've explored in previous chapters, Secure Access Service Edge (SASE) is a networking model that converges network and security services into a single, cloud-native architecture. SASE is all about providing secure, high-performance access to cloud resources from any device, anywhere. And this is where ZTNA comes into the picture.

ZTNA is a perfect match for SASE because it provides the granular, identity-based access control that SASE requires. In the SASE model, it's not enough to simply secure the network perimeter – you must also secure each individual application. That's where ZTNA shines.

By integrating ZTNA into the SASE framework, organizations can ensure that every access request is thoroughly authenticated and authorized, no matter where it originates or where the application resides. This delivers a level of security that traditional network-centric approaches can't match, while also providing a smoother user experience.

ZTNA and the Future of Work

The ongoing pandemic has radically reshaped our ideas of what a workplace looks like. With the rise of remote work, employees are no longer tied to a physical office – they can work from home, a coffee shop, or a beach halfway across the world.

This shift has major implications for network security. The traditional, perimeter-based model is ill-suited for this new reality. It's simply not feasible to secure every home network, public Wi-Fi hotspot, or remote desktop.

But ZTNA is designed for exactly this kind of scenario. By focusing on securing individual applications rather than entire networks, ZTNA can provide secure access to remote workers no matter where they are or what device they're using.

In conclusion, ZTNA is more than just a security solution. It's a fundamental rethinking of how we approach network security in the age of cloud and mobility. And as we move further into this new era, ZTNA – and by extension, SASE – will only become more important.

ZTNA in Practice - Case Studies

To bring these concepts to life, let's take a look at a few case studies where ZTNA has made a significant difference in organizations.

Healthcare Provider: Managing Sensitive Data

A healthcare provider needed to ensure that its network of hospitals, clinics, and other facilities had secure access to patient data. The traditional VPN solutions they were using were unable to provide the level of granular control they needed. By implementing a ZTNA solution, the healthcare provider was able to ensure that only authorized personnel could access patient records, and only from secure, compliant devices.

Manufacturing Firm: Securing Intellectual Property

A global manufacturing firm needed to protect its sensitive intellectual property from potential cyber threats. Their conventional network security was insufficient against advanced persistent threats that could bypass perimeter defenses. With ZTNA, they were able to secure access to their sensitive design and manufacturing systems, greatly reducing the risk of data breaches.

Education Institution: Remote Learning Security

A large university had to quickly shift to remote learning due to the pandemic. This sudden change exposed vulnerabilities in their network security, as students and staff were now accessing resources from a wide range of locations and devices. Implementing a ZTNA solution allowed the university to ensure secure access to learning resources, regardless of the user's location.

Common ZTNA Challenges and How to Overcome Them

While the benefits of ZTNA are numerous, implementing it can present certain challenges. Here are some common hurdles organizations face and how they can be overcome:

1. Complexity: Implementing ZTNA can be complex due to its granular nature. It's essential to take a step-by-step approach, starting with the most sensitive applications, and gradually extending ZTNA across the organization.
2. User resistance: As with any new technology, there can be resistance from users. To overcome this, focus on communicating the benefits of ZTNA - not just for the organization, but for the users themselves (e.g., flexibility, accessibility).
3. Choosing the right solution: There are many ZTNA solutions in the market, and choosing the right one can be a challenge. It's important to consider factors like the solution's integration capabilities, scalability, and customer support.

A Step-by-step Guide to ZTNA Implementation

To conclude our deep-dive into ZTNA, let's end with a step-by-step guide that can serve as a roadmap to implementing ZTNA in your organization.

Step 1: Define Your Security Objectives

Identify the key security objectives that ZTNA will help you achieve. This might include protecting sensitive data, securing remote access, or improving visibility and control over network traffic.

Step 2: Identify Key Applications

Identify the applications that are most critical to your business operations, or that handle the most sensitive data. These are the applications you should start with when implementing ZTNA.

Step 3: Define Access Policies

For each identified application, define who should have access, under what circumstances, and with what level of privileges. These policies should be defined based on the principle of least privilege.

Step 4: Choose the Right ZTNA Solution

Consider your specific needs and constraints when choosing a ZTNA solution. The best solution for your organization will depend on a variety of factors, including your network architecture, the nature of your applications, and your budget.

Step 5: Pilot and Refine

Before rolling out ZTNA across your entire organization, start with a pilot project. Use the feedback and insights gained from the pilot to refine your approach and address any issues before moving forward.

Step 6: Train and Educate

Educate your employees about ZTNA, why it's being implemented, and how it will affect them. Provide training on how to use any new tools or processes that are part of the ZTNA solution.

Step 7: Rollout and Monitor

Once you're ready to implement ZTNA more broadly, begin a phased rollout. Monitor the implementation closely to identify any issues or areas for improvement.

ZTNA and Compliance

The implementation of ZTNA can also have significant implications for regulatory compliance. Many industries have strict regulations concerning data privacy and security, such as the Health Insurance Portability and Accountability Act (HIPAA) in healthcare or the General Data Protection Regulation (GDPR) in the European Union.

With its robust access controls and detailed logging capabilities, ZTNA can play a key role in meeting these compliance requirements. By ensuring that only authorized users can access sensitive data, and by providing a detailed audit trail of who accessed what and when, ZTNA can help organizations demonstrate their compliance with regulatory requirements.

ZTNA: Not a Panacea, But a Vital Component

While ZTNA offers many benefits, it's important to remember that no single technology can provide complete security. ZTNA should be seen as one component of a multi-layered security strategy that might include other technologies such as firewalls, intrusion detection systems, endpoint protection platforms, and more.

The Road Ahead for ZTNA

Looking ahead, the future of ZTNA looks promising. As more organizations embrace the cloud, remote work, and digital transformation, the need for solutions like ZTNA will only grow.

While the technology is still evolving, it's clear that ZTNA – along with the broader SASE framework – represents a significant step forward in the way we approach network security. It provides a flexible, scalable, and secure solution that is well-suited to the demands of the modern digital landscape.

The Interplay between ZTNA and Other Security Technologies

Understanding how ZTNA fits in with the other security technologies in your stack is essential for creating an effective and comprehensive security strategy.

Firewalls and ZTNA

At first glance, ZTNA might seem to make traditional firewalls obsolete. However, while ZTNA does address some of the limitations of traditional firewalls, it does not replace them completely. Firewalls are still necessary for protecting the network perimeter and filtering out malicious traffic.

Endpoint Security and ZTNA

Endpoint security solutions protect individual devices (the endpoints) from threats. When combined with ZTNA, you can add another layer of security by ensuring not just that the device is secure, but also that any access request it sends is properly authenticated and authorized.

Secure Web Gateways and ZTNA

Secure web gateways (SWGs) provide security and control for internet-bound traffic. They're complementary to ZTNA because while SWGs protect against internet-based threats, ZTNA protects applications from unauthorized access.

The Future of ZTNA - Predictions and Trends

As we look to the future, it's clear that ZTNA is not just a passing trend, but a fundamental shift in how we approach network security.

AI and Machine Learning

Expect to see artificial intelligence (AI) and machine learning (ML) playing a bigger role in ZTNA solutions. These technologies can help automate and enhance the decision-making process for access requests, making ZTNA more efficient and effective.

More Granular Controls

As ZTNA technology matures, expect to see more granular controls and more sophisticated policy options. This will allow organizations to tailor their ZTNA implementation more closely to their specific needs and risk tolerance.

Integration with Other Security Technologies

As mentioned earlier, ZTNA is most effective when integrated with other security technologies. Expect to see more out-of-the-box integrations between ZTNA solutions and other security tools, making it easier for organizations to implement a multi-layered security strategy.

Greater Adoption

As more organizations see the benefits of ZTNA, adoption will continue to increase. According to Gartner, by 2023, 60% of enterprises will phase out most of their remote access virtual private networks (VPNs) in favor of ZTNA.

It's clear that ZTNA, as part of the broader SASE framework, is here to stay. Embracing it is not just a matter of keeping up with the latest tech trends—it's about safeguarding the future of your organization.

I hope you have found this deep dive into ZTNA informative and useful. In the next chapter, we will be shifting our focus to another important aspect of SASE: Secure Web Gateways (SWGs). Stay tuned!

Chapter 8: Secure Web Gateways Explained

SWGs have come to play a pivotal role in securing organizational networks. As the name suggests, Secure Web Gateways (SWGs) serve as a gatekeeper between users and the internet, ensuring that the traffic flowing between the two is safe and within the company's policy guidelines.

Why do we need Secure Web Gateways?

In today's digital landscape, internet-based threats are becoming increasingly sophisticated. It's no longer enough to rely on traditional security measures like firewalls and antivirus software. With the widespread adoption of cloud-based services, mobile computing, and remote work, a significant portion of an organization's traffic now involves users accessing the internet or cloud-based applications.

This shift has created a pressing need for a solution that can provide robust protection against web-based threats, while also ensuring compliance with company policies - and that's where SWGs come in.

How do Secure Web Gateways work?

SWGs work by intercepting and inspecting all web traffic that flows between users and the internet. This includes traffic initiated by the user, such as browsing activity, as well as traffic initiated from the internet, such as incoming emails or downloads.

The inspection process involves several steps. First, the SWG uses URL filtering to block access to blacklisted or inappropriate websites. It then scans the remaining traffic for malware using various detection techniques. Finally, it applies content and application control policies to ensure that the traffic complies with company policies.

Understanding Key SWG Features

Let's delve deeper into the primary features of SWGs:

1. URL Filtering: SWGs maintain a database of URLs categorized based on their content, security status, and reputation. This allows the SWG to block or allow access to websites based on these categories.

2. Malware Detection: SWGs use several methods to detect malware, including signature-based detection, heuristic analysis, and sandboxing.

3. Application Control: SWGs can identify and control the use of various web-based applications, including social media, instant messaging, and file sharing services.

4. Data Loss Prevention (DLP): Some SWGs include DLP capabilities to prevent sensitive data from being transmitted outside the organization.

5. Mobile and Remote User Support: Many SWGs offer features designed specifically for mobile and remote users, such as clientless operation and integration with other security solutions.

Implementing Secure Web Gateways - A Step-by-step Approach

Implementing SWGs involves several steps, each crucial in ensuring a smooth transition and maximum security.

Step 1: Define Your Requirements

First, identify your organization's specific needs. These might include the type of threats you face, the nature of your internet traffic, your policy enforcement needs, and your legal and regulatory requirements.

Step 2: Evaluate Different Solutions

Next, evaluate different SWG solutions based on your defined requirements. Consider factors such as the solution's feature set, its performance, its scalability, and its ease of use.

Step 3: Test the Solution

Before deploying the solution company-wide, test it in a limited environment. This will allow you to identify any potential issues or gaps in coverage, as well as gain a better understanding of how the solution works.

Step 4: Deploy the Solution

After testing, you can begin to deploy the solution across your organization. Depending on your organization's size and complexity, this might involve a phased approach.

Step 5: Monitor and Adjust

Once the SWG is deployed, monitor its performance and make any necessary adjustments. This might involve tweaking your policies, adding new URL categories, or adjusting your malware detection settings.

The Role of SWGs in a SASE Architecture

SWGs play a crucial role in a SASE architecture. Within SASE, SWGs provide the security component for web-based traffic. They work alongside other SASE components such as SD-WAN and ZTNA to provide a comprehensive, flexible, and scalable security solution that is well-suited to the needs of modern organizations.

Digging Deeper: Advanced SWG Features

For a more technical perspective, let's unpack some advanced SWG features:

1. Advanced Threat Protection (ATP): ATP goes beyond traditional malware detection, using techniques like behavioral analysis and sandboxing to identify and block zero-day threats and advanced persistent threats (APTs).

2. SSL Inspection: As more and more web traffic becomes encrypted using SSL/TLS, SWGs need to be able to inspect this encrypted traffic for threats. SSL inspection involves decrypting the traffic, scanning it for threats, and then re-encrypting it.

3. Integration with Other Security Solutions: Many SWGs can integrate with other security solutions, such as firewalls, intrusion prevention systems (IPS), and security information and event management (SIEM) systems. This allows for coordinated threat response and comprehensive security analytics.

SWGs and the Cloud: A Perfect Match?

The cloud has become a game-changer for many facets of IT, and network security is no exception. SWGs are increasingly being delivered as a cloud service, which provides several benefits:

1. Scalability: Cloud-based SWGs can easily scale up or down to accommodate changes in your web traffic, providing cost-effective flexibility.

2. Simplicity: Implementing a cloud-based SWG is generally simpler than deploying an on-premise solution. There's no hardware to install, and updates and patches are handled automatically.

3. Performance: Cloud-based SWGs can provide better performance, particularly for remote users or offices, as they can connect directly to the nearest SWG data center.

However, like with any cloud service, organizations need to consider potential issues like data privacy and regulatory compliance when implementing a cloud-based SWG.

The Intricacies of SSL Inspection

We briefly touched on SSL inspection earlier, but this feature merits a deeper dive due to its importance in today's digital landscape. With most web traffic now encrypted using SSL or TLS, the ability to inspect this traffic is critical to catching threats that might be hiding within it.

SSL inspection involves several steps. First, the SWG intercepts the SSL connection and presents its own certificate to the client, effectively establishing an SSL connection between the client and the SWG. Next, it establishes another SSL connection with the server. This allows the SWG to decrypt and inspect the traffic as it passes through.

However, SSL inspection is not without its challenges. It's a resource-intensive process that can impact network performance if not managed properly. Additionally, it raises privacy concerns, as it essentially involves a 'man-in-the-middle' approach where the SWG can see all traffic, including potentially sensitive information.

Role of AI and Machine Learning in SWGs

Artificial intelligence (AI) and machine learning (ML) are increasingly being used in SWGs to improve threat detection capabilities. By learning from historical traffic patterns, these technologies can identify anomalous behavior that may indicate a threat. They can also help in detecting zero-day threats, which are new or previously unknown threats that traditional signature-based detection methods might miss.

SWGs and Regulatory Compliance

SWGs can play a crucial role in helping organizations meet their regulatory compliance obligations. Many regulations, such as the General Data Protection Regulation (GDPR) and the Health Insurance Portability and Accountability Act (HIPAA), have strict requirements concerning data privacy and security. By providing robust control over web traffic and detailed logging capabilities, SWGs can help organizations demonstrate their compliance with these regulations.

Decoding Advanced Threat Protection (ATP) in SWGs

Advanced Threat Protection (ATP) is a paramount feature in SWGs that elevates their malware detection capabilities. ATP combines a multitude of techniques such as behavioral analysis, sandboxing, and reputation analysis to combat increasingly sophisticated threats. For instance, behavioral analysis and sandboxing help detect zero-day threats, which are new and unknown threats that evade traditional signature-based detection.

Behavioral analysis involves examining the behavior of files to identify activities that could indicate a threat, while sandboxing involves running potentially malicious files in an isolated environment to observe their behavior. Reputation analysis, on the other hand, evaluates files based on their reputation score calculated from various factors like their source, prevalence, age, etc.

The Future of SWGs - Machine Learning and Predictive Analysis

As technology progresses, so do SWGs. The future of SWGs is already being shaped by machine learning and predictive analysis. With these technologies, SWGs will be able to anticipate and neutralize threats even before they strike. For instance, predictive analysis can anticipate a cyber-attack based on patterns observed in past attacks, while machine learning algorithms can automatically adapt to evolving threat landscapes.

Unpacking SSL Decryption – The Heart of SSL Inspection

As web traffic continues to be heavily encrypted with Secure Socket Layer (SSL) or Transport Layer Security

(TLS), SSL decryption becomes vital to a Secure Web Gateway's function. It enables the SWG to inspect the contents of encrypted traffic for possible threats.

However, decrypting SSL traffic isn't as straightforward as it sounds. It requires resource-intensive computation and careful handling to maintain user privacy and trust. During decryption, the SWG intercepts the SSL/TLS handshake between the client and the server. It then inserts itself into the conversation by presenting its own certificate to the client. This way, the SWG establishes two separate SSL/TLS connections: one with the client and the other with the server. This setup enables the SWG to decrypt, inspect, and re-encrypt the traffic without breaking the secure communication.

It's worth noting that SSL decryption poses a challenge to organizations due to its high computational cost, which can impact network performance. Moreover, it raises ethical and legal questions about user privacy, since it involves deciphering encrypted data that may contain sensitive information.

The Emerging Role of AI and Machine Learning in SWGs

Artificial Intelligence (AI) and Machine Learning (ML) have started revolutionizing various aspects of technology, and Secure Web Gateways are no exception. Incorporating AI and ML into SWGs brings several advantages, especially in terms of threat detection and response.

AI and ML are excellent at pattern recognition. By analyzing historical network traffic data, these algorithms can learn to identify patterns of normal behavior. Once they have a baseline of what's considered 'normal,' they can detect anomalous traffic patterns that may indicate a potential security threat. This ability becomes increasingly useful in detecting zero-day exploits and advanced persistent threats that do not have known signatures.

Moreover, machine learning can continually improve SWG's threat detection capabilities. As it is exposed to more data over time, it can refine its models and improve its accuracy, helping organizations stay ahead of the ever-evolving cyber threat landscape.

Secure Web Gateways and Regulatory Compliance – A Match Made in Heaven

Maintaining regulatory compliance is a significant concern for many businesses, especially those in heavily regulated sectors like healthcare and finance. Here, Secure Web Gateways can prove to be invaluable.

Regulations such as the GDPR, HIPAA, or PCI-DSS impose stringent requirements concerning data security and privacy. Non-compliance can result in hefty fines and reputational damage. SWGs help organizations comply with these regulations by providing robust control over their web traffic and preventing unauthorized data transmission. The detailed logging and reporting capabilities of SWGs provide auditable evidence of compliance, a crucial feature when demonstrating regulatory adherence.

Unravelling Sandboxing – A Key Mechanism in ATP

Sandboxing is an essential component of Advanced Threat Protection in Secure Web Gateways, aimed at detecting new and unknown threats that conventional security measures might overlook. But what exactly is sandboxing, and how does it work?

At its core, sandboxing involves creating an isolated, secure environment in which to execute and observe potentially malicious files. By running these files in a sandbox, SWGs can safely monitor their behavior without risking the broader network's security. If the file acts maliciously - for instance, by attempting to make unauthorized network connections or modify system files - the SWG can detect this behavior and prevent the file from causing harm in the real environment.

Though effective, sandboxing is not without challenges. It's resource-intensive and can introduce latency into network operations, especially when handling large volumes of traffic. SWG solutions are continually evolving to address these challenges and ensure efficient, effective sandboxing that doesn't compromise network performance.

Secure Web Gateways and the Emergence of Deep Learning

Deep Learning, a subset of machine learning, is beginning to find its place in the realm of SWGs, promising even more advanced threat detection capabilities. While traditional machine learning relies on manually designed feature extraction, deep learning models can automatically learn to represent data by training on large volumes of data. This automated feature extraction enables deep learning models to identify more complex patterns and anomalies, significantly enhancing their threat detection capabilities.

In the context of SWGs, deep learning could enable more accurate detection of zero-day exploits and advanced persistent threats. It could also improve the effectiveness of data loss prevention by identifying subtle patterns of data misuse. As deep learning models continue to improve and mature, we can expect to see them play an increasingly significant role in SWG technology.

The Road Ahead – Secure Web Gateways in the Era of SASE

As we look to the future, the role of Secure Web Gateways within the Secure Access Service Edge (SASE) architecture becomes increasingly vital. SASE, with its emphasis on integrating networking and security services into a single cloud-based service, is a perfect fit for SWGs.

SWGs in a SASE architecture offer several advantages, including simplified management, improved scalability, and enhanced security. They provide organizations with a unified security platform that can protect users regardless of their location – a critical feature in today's era of remote work and cloud services.

The future of SWGs within SASE will likely involve even greater integration with other security services, further enhancing their capabilities and ease of management. As technology continues to advance, SWGs will continue to evolve, offering ever more powerful and flexible solutions to the challenges of securing web traffic.

Diving Deeper into Data Loss Prevention

Data Loss Prevention (DLP) is a feature of Secure Web Gateways that is particularly significant in today's business landscape. With sensitive corporate and customer data flowing through network systems, DLP is paramount in preventing this information from falling into the wrong hands.

In essence, DLP is all about identifying, monitoring, and protecting data in use, data in motion, and data at rest. Using rules and policies, DLP systems can detect potential data breaches or data exfiltration transmissions and prevent them by monitoring data while in use, in motion, and at rest.

However, setting up effective DLP policies requires a deep understanding of the organization's data flows, classification of sensitive data, and applicable regulations. It's a complex task that demands careful planning and meticulous implementation. The implementation of machine learning and artificial intelligence can significantly ease this process by automating the classification of data and identifying suspicious patterns.

SWGs and Endpoint Protection

An often-underappreciated facet of SWGs is their role in endpoint protection. Endpoints, such as laptops, smartphones, and tablets, are often the weakest link in an organization's security chain. SWGs help safeguard these devices by controlling their access to potentially harmful websites and ensuring that any web-based threats do not reach the endpoints.

By blocking access to malicious websites, SWGs can prevent endpoints from becoming infected with malware. Moreover, by scanning incoming traffic for threats, they can stop malware and other attacks before they reach the endpoints. The use of advanced threat protection mechanisms, such as sandboxing and behavior-based detection, further enhances their endpoint protection capabilities.

Looking to the Future - SWGs in a Zero Trust World

As we move towards a zero trust model of security, where trust is never assumed and always verified, the role of SWGs becomes even more critical. In a zero trust model, every access request is fully authenticated, authorized, and encrypted before access is granted.

In such a landscape, SWGs will become an essential tool in the verification process. By examining all web traffic, regardless of its source, SWGs can help ensure that only legitimate, authorized requests are allowed. They can also provide an additional layer of security by scanning this traffic for potential threats.

This bring us into the importance of Intrusion Prevention Systems.

Chapter 9: An Introduction to Intrusion Prevention Systems (IPS)

The digital landscape is evolving at a rapid pace, and so are the cybersecurity threats that come along with it. Businesses and organizations are continually seeking effective solutions to safeguard their digital assets and operations. Enter Intrusion Prevention Systems (IPS).

An IPS is a critical tool in the cybersecurity arsenal. It monitors network traffic for malicious activities or security policy violations and attempts to block them before they cause harm. Now, what happens when we integrate an IPS into a Secure Access Service Edge (SASE) architecture? You get a holistic, cloud-native, location-independent security solution that brings together the best of networking and security services.

SASE is all about delivering network security from the cloud, decoupling it from specific hardware devices and allowing it to be as dynamic and flexible as the networks it is designed to protect. When IPS is embedded within a SASE framework, it leverages the cloud's scalability and omnipresence to offer a more robust, flexible, and proactive defense mechanism.

Understanding IPS - From Basics to Advanced Features

Before we dive into the intricacies of an IPS within SASE, it's vital to comprehend the basic functioning of an IPS. An IPS continually monitors your network traffic and analyzes it for any potential threats or irregularities. When it identifies a threat, it acts by blocking the malicious traffic or alerting system administrators.

However, modern IPS solutions are not just about identifying and blocking threats - they are far more sophisticated. Many IPS solutions employ advanced features such as behavior-based detection, anomaly detection, and signature-based detection. Furthermore, some IPS solutions also integrate with machine learning and artificial intelligence technologies to better identify and respond to emerging threats.

The Role of IPS in a SASE Architecture

In a SASE architecture, the IPS takes on a crucial role. It forms a core part of the integrated security framework that SASE offers, providing essential protection against network-based attacks. Being cloud-native, the IPS in a SASE context can monitor and protect network traffic regardless of where it originates - be it an on-premises data center, a remote worker, or a cloud service.

Unpacking Signature-Based Detection in IPS

Signature-based detection is one of the foundational pillars of an Intrusion Prevention System. Simply put, it's akin to a detective looking for a known criminal's fingerprints at a crime scene. In this case, the 'crime scene' is your network, and the 'fingerprints' are specific patterns of data or 'signatures' that are indicative of malicious activity.

IPS solutions come equipped with a database of these signatures, which are continually updated to incorporate the latest threats. When network traffic matches a known signature, the IPS raises the alarm and takes the necessary action to prevent any harm. However, it's important to note that while signature-based detection is powerful for catching known threats, it has limitations when dealing with zero-day threats or highly customized attacks.

The Power of Anomaly Detection in IPS

To address the limitations of signature-based detection, many modern IPS solutions employ anomaly detection. This technique involves establishing a baseline of 'normal' network behavior, and then monitoring for deviations from this baseline that might indicate malicious activity.

In a SASE context, anomaly detection becomes even more potent. Given that SASE architectures are cloud-native and can ingest and analyze massive amounts of data, they can develop a far more nuanced understanding of 'normal' behavior. This enhanced understanding can improve the accuracy of anomaly detection, allowing for more precise identification of malicious activities.

Behaviour-Based Detection – Unmasking the Unknown

Taking things up a notch, behavior-based detection adds another layer of sophistication to IPS in a SASE context. This technique doesn't just rely on known signatures or deviations from a baseline. Instead, it monitors the behavior of network traffic to identify actions that might indicate a security threat.

For instance, a file that tries to modify system files or connect to a known malicious IP address would be flagged by a behavior-based detection system, even if it didn't match any known signatures or represented a significant deviation from normal network traffic. In a SASE context, behavior-based detection can leverage the power of the cloud to analyze vast amounts of data in real-time, enhancing its threat detection capabilities.

Harnessing AI and Machine Learning in IPS

One of the most significant advancements in Intrusion Prevention Systems comes from harnessing the power of Artificial Intelligence (AI) and Machine Learning (ML). By integrating these technologies into IPS within a SASE architecture, we can create a more adaptive, intelligent, and effective security solution.

AI and ML bring several key enhancements to IPS. Firstly, they can improve threat detection accuracy. By learning from vast amounts of data, AI and ML can identify patterns and anomalies that humans or traditional systems might overlook. They can also predict emerging threats by identifying patterns that precede an attack, enabling proactive defense.

Secondly, AI and ML can automate and accelerate threat response. They can analyze threats in real-time and take immediate action to mitigate them, such as blocking a malicious IP or quarantining a compromised device. This rapid response can limit the damage caused by security incidents and reduce their remediation time and cost.

In a SASE context, the integration of AI and ML with IPS becomes even more potent. The cloud-native nature of SASE allows AI and ML to leverage virtually limitless computing resources to analyze data and respond to threats. Moreover, the integrated nature of SASE means that the AI and ML can act on insights from other parts of the SASE architecture, enhancing their effectiveness.

The Evolution of IPS in SASE – Looking Towards the Future

As we move forward into an increasingly digital, cloud-based world, the role of IPS within a SASE architecture will only continue to grow in importance. We're already witnessing advancements that leverage AI and ML, and we can expect these to continue, driving more powerful and intelligent IPS solutions.

Moreover, as networking and security become more intertwined, IPS solutions will increasingly need to work in harmony with other parts of the SASE architecture. They will need to share insights and coordinate responses with other components, such as Secure Web Gateways and Zero Trust Network Access solutions. This level of integration will drive more holistic, effective security solutions that can protect against the evolving threat landscape.

Finally, the shift towards remote work and cloud services will necessitate more flexible and scalable IPS solutions. SASE, with its cloud-native, location-independent architecture, is ideally suited to meet these needs. By delivering IPS from the cloud, SASE can provide robust security that scales with your network and adapts to its changing needs.

Scaling IPS with SASE – Meeting the Demands of the Modern Workforce

Modern workforces are more distributed and mobile than ever before. Workers are no longer confined to a physical office; they can work from anywhere, using any device. This flexibility has brought tremendous benefits in terms of productivity and work-life balance, but it has also introduced new security challenges. These challenges call for an IPS that can keep up - an IPS that is as flexible and dynamic as the workforce it protects.

SASE is ideally suited to meet these needs. By delivering IPS from the cloud, SASE can ensure that every connection, no matter where it originates, is subject to the same level of scrutiny and protection. Remote workers connecting from home or public Wi-Fi, applications running in the cloud, IoT devices scattered across multiple locations - all are protected by the IPS within a SASE framework.

But SASE does more than just make IPS more accessible; it also makes it more scalable. As your workforce grows or shrinks, as your network expands or contracts, your SASE-based IPS can adapt. The cloud's virtually limitless resources mean that you can scale your IPS capabilities up or down as needed, ensuring that you always have the right level of protection without overpaying for resources you don't need.

SASE and IPS - Ensuring Compliance and Governance

In today's world, organizations are subject to a myriad of regulations and standards related to cybersecurity. Failure to comply with these can result in hefty fines, reputational damage, and loss of customer trust. An IPS within a SASE framework can play a critical role in ensuring compliance and governance.

SASE's ability to monitor and log all network activity is a valuable asset in demonstrating compliance. It can provide a detailed, auditable record of all network transactions, allowing you to show regulators that you have taken the necessary steps to protect your network.

Additionally, the advanced threat detection capabilities of an IPS within SASE can help you meet specific regulatory requirements. For example, regulations such as the GDPR and CCPA require organizations to protect personal data. The IPS can help ensure that this data is not being accessed or transmitted without authorization, thereby aiding in compliance.

Enhancing Visibility with IPS in SASE

One of the significant advantages of integrating IPS into a SASE architecture is the enhanced visibility it provides. Visibility is a cornerstone of effective cybersecurity - you can't protect what you can't see. In a traditional network setup, gaining complete visibility can be challenging due to multiple standalone security solutions and network components. However, the integration of security and networking that SASE offers eliminates these silos, providing a unified view of your network.

Within the SASE framework, the IPS provides detailed insights into network traffic, highlighting potential threats and security incidents in real-time. It illuminates the corners of your network that might otherwise remain in shadow, such as remote worker connections or cloud services. By doing so, it ensures that all aspects of your network remain under your watchful eye.

Additionally, the data gathered by the IPS can be used to improve other components of your SASE solution. For example, it can feed into your Zero Trust Network Access solution, helping it make more informed decisions about access requests. It can also assist in the fine-tuning of your Secure Web Gateway, helping it better identify and block harmful web content.

The Power of Context in IPS and SASE

Context is an essential factor in modern cybersecurity. Knowing who is making a connection, where they're connecting from, what they're trying to connect to, and how they're trying to connect can provide valuable insights that inform security decisions. In a SASE architecture, the IPS can take full advantage of this context.

The IPS within a SASE solution can use context to more accurately identify threats. For example, a large file transfer might be normal for a data backup process but suspicious for a standard user account. By understanding the context, the IPS can distinguish between these scenarios and respond accordingly.

Furthermore, the context can also be used to minimize the impact of security measures on legitimate traffic. By understanding what 'normal' looks like for different users and applications, the IPS can tailor its policies to provide security without hindering productivity. But it's not just IPS which helps us in the world of SASE security, there's also anti-malware to worry about.

Chapter 10: The rise of Anti-Malware

The digital frontier is an ever-evolving landscape, marked by the steady progression of technology and the corresponding emergence of new threats. As cyber attackers become more sophisticated and devious, the tools we use to defend our networks must evolve too. One such tool that has seen significant advancements in recent years is anti-malware software, specifically its next-generation iterations. These advancements take center stage when discussing Secure Access Service Edge (SASE) – a security model that brings together networking and security in a unified, cloud-based solution.

Traditionally, anti-malware software was designed to detect known threats using signature-based techniques. It compared files to a database of known malware signatures, and if a match was found, the file was flagged as malicious. While this approach was effective against known threats, it struggled to detect new, unknown threats, such as zero-day exploits. This limitation led to the development of next-generation anti-malware, which uses more sophisticated techniques to identify and block threats.

Next-generation anti-malware integrates multiple approaches to threat detection. In addition to signature-based techniques, it leverages behavior-based detection, which monitors the behavior of files and programs to detect suspicious activity. For instance, if a seemingly benign file attempts to modify critical system files, behavior-based detection would flag this as suspicious, even if the file's signature doesn't match any known threats. Next-generation anti-malware also employs heuristics, which look for general patterns of malicious activity rather than specific signatures.

Moreover, next-generation anti-malware often integrates artificial intelligence (AI) and machine learning (ML) to enhance its threat detection capabilities. By learning from past threats, these technologies can identify new threats more accurately, even ones that don't match any known signatures or behaviors. AI and ML also enable proactive threat detection, allowing the anti-malware to identify and block threats before they can cause harm.

Now, let's consider how these advancements in anti-malware fit into the SASE architecture. SASE is all about delivering security from the cloud, allowing it to be as dynamic and scalable as the networks it protects. When next-generation anti-malware is integrated into a SASE solution, it benefits from the cloud's scalability and flexibility. This cloud-native approach allows the anti-malware to protect all aspects of a network, regardless of where they are located – whether it's a remote worker's laptop, an on-premises server, or a cloud-based application.

Furthermore, SASE's integrated approach to networking and security allows next-generation anti-malware to work in harmony with other security components. For instance, it can share insights with the intrusion prevention system (IPS) to better identify threats, or coordinate with the secure web gateway (SWG) to block harmful web content.

Having the combined capabilities of different security components in a SASE model allows your next-generation anti-malware to perform at a higher level. It allows for threat intelligence sharing across various components of the system, creating a more resilient security posture. One particular advantage of this interoperability is the potential for correlation of events across different security layers. For instance, a seemingly innocuous event picked up by the SWG could be correlated with a suspicious file detected by the anti-malware, revealing an ongoing attack that would otherwise be missed.

Furthermore, a SASE model leverages the power of the cloud for threat intelligence. With traditional, on-premises anti-malware, updating malware signatures and behavioral patterns could take a significant amount of time, especially for organizations with a large number of endpoints. In the time it takes for these updates to be rolled out, a new malware could cause significant damage. However, with SASE, these updates can be made almost instantaneously, ensuring your network is protected against the latest threats at all times.

The cloud-native nature of SASE also enables scalability and flexibility in dealing with threats. With traditional anti-malware, an increase in traffic could overwhelm your defenses, making them less effective. In contrast, with SASE, your anti-malware capabilities can scale with your network traffic, ensuring consistent protection even during peak loads. It also allows you to tailor your security based on user roles and locations. For instance, you can enforce stricter controls for high-risk users or sensitive applications, providing a level of granular control that is difficult to achieve with traditional anti-malware.

There's also an advantage when it comes to incident response and remediation. The integration and consolidation of different security services in a SASE model can expedite the response to security incidents. If the anti-malware detects a threat, it can immediately alert other components of the system, which can then take action to mitigate the threat. This coordinated response can significantly reduce the potential damage of security incidents.

Another significant advantage of the integration of next-generation anti-malware into the SASE architecture is the centralized visibility and control it offers. With traditional security solutions, you may have to sift through multiple, disjointed security logs to gain a comprehensive understanding of a security incident. However, within a SASE framework, all security events are logged in a centralized location. This consolidated view makes it easier to spot trends, identify root causes, and make informed decisions.

Centralized control also simplifies the management of security policies. Instead of configuring multiple standalone anti-malware solutions, you can define policies centrally and propagate them across the entire network. This centralized management not only saves time but also ensures consistency in your security policies, reducing the chances of misconfigurations that can lead to security gaps.

Furthermore, SASE's cloud-native nature provides an opportunity for continuous updates and innovation. As new threats emerge and the security landscape evolves, your next-generation anti-malware solution can be updated and enhanced in the cloud without any disruption to your network. This ensures your defenses stay up-to-date with the latest advancements in threat detection and prevention.

In addition to these operational benefits, there are also cost implications to consider. By integrating next-generation anti-malware into a SASE solution, you can potentially reduce the total cost of ownership (TCO). You save on hardware costs, as there's no need for dedicated anti-malware appliances. There's also less overhead for management and maintenance, as these tasks are handled by the SASE provider. Plus, the pay-as-you-go model of most cloud services means you only pay for what you use, allowing you to scale your costs with your needs.

What's the Difference Between Anti-Malware and Next-Generation Anti-Malware?

In the world of cybersecurity, evolution is constant. Cyber threats are incessantly growing in number and complexity, requiring us to continually innovate and adapt our defense mechanisms. This never-ending race has birthed the concept of next-generation anti-malware – a term that tech professionals and security enthusiasts alike often come across. So, what distinguishes next-generation anti-malware from traditional anti-malware? Let's delve into the specifics.

Traditional anti-malware operates predominantly on the basis of signature detection. It maintains a vast database of malware signatures – unique identifying characteristics of known malware. When a file enters your system, the anti-malware checks it against this database. If there's a match, it's flagged as malicious and dealt with accordingly. However, this approach is not without its shortcomings. It's great for dealing with known threats, but completely impotent against new, previously unseen malware, also known as zero-day threats.

In contrast, next-generation anti-malware is engineered to tackle this very issue. It leverages a myriad of more sophisticated techniques that allow it to identify and deal with both known and unknown threats. One of these techniques is behavioral detection. This method monitors the behavior of programs and files in real-time. If a file begins to behave suspiciously – attempting to modify system files or make unusual network connections, for instance – it is identified as a potential threat, even if it has never been seen before.

Next-generation anti-malware also utilizes machine learning and artificial intelligence to improve its threat detection capabilities. Machine learning allows the software to learn from past instances of malware, improving its ability to detect new threats. AI, on the other hand, enhances the software's predictive capabilities, helping it identify and neutralize threats even before they strike.

Another key difference lies in the area of threat response. Traditional anti-malware typically takes a binary approach – a file is either malicious and hence deleted or quarantined, or it's benign and left alone. Next-generation anti-malware, however, takes a more nuanced approach. Depending on the severity of the threat, it might choose to simply monitor a suspicious file, restrict its access to certain system resources, or prevent it from executing altogether.

As a technical professional, understanding these differences is crucial. As our digital landscapes continue to evolve and new threats continue to emerge, so too must our defenses. Next-generation anti-malware is not just an upgrade to traditional anti-malware; it's a fundamental shift towards a more proactive, intelligent, and nuanced approach to cybersecurity – an approach befitting the complexities of today's digital world.

Diving Deeper: Signature-Based vs. Heuristic Detection

As we delve further into the technological intricacies of anti-malware strategies, it's essential to understand the different methodologies that software employs to detect and combat threats. Two key techniques in this domain are signature-based detection and heuristic detection. Both are crucial in the fight against malware, but they operate on fundamentally different principles and are effective against different types of threats.

Signature-Based Detection

Signature-based detection is the older, more traditional method of the two. It operates by comparing files and programs against a vast database of known malware signatures. A malware signature is a unique pattern or string of code that serves as a sort of 'fingerprint' for a specific piece of malware. When you run a scan with signature-based anti-malware, it checks every file and program on your system against its database. If it finds a match, it flags the file as malicious.

The strength of signature-based detection lies in its reliability when it comes to identifying known threats. It's tried-and-true and highly effective against malware that has been seen before. However, its weakness becomes apparent when it encounters new, unknown threats, commonly known as zero-day threats. Because these threats don't yet have a known signature, they can slip past signature-based defenses unnoticed.

Heuristic Detection

This is where heuristic detection comes into play. Heuristic detection doesn't just look for known signatures; instead, it analyzes the behavior and characteristics of files and programs to identify potential threats. It looks for suspicious patterns, such as attempts to access protected system areas, the use of packers or obfuscators (tools that can be used to hide malware), and other potentially dangerous behaviors.

This approach allows heuristic detection to identify unknown threats that would go unnoticed by signature-based detection. It can even catch new variants of known malware, provided they exhibit similar behaviors. However, heuristic detection is not without its drawbacks. Its proactive approach can sometimes lead to false positives, flagging benign files as potentially harmful. Therefore, it requires more computational resources and might slow down system performance.

In the grand scheme of things, it's not a question of which technique is better overall. Instead, the choice between signature-based and heuristic detection is about finding the right balance. In an ideal world, your anti-malware solution would use both methods: signature-based detection for its proven reliability against known threats, and heuristic detection for its ability to catch new and evolving malware. The interplay of these two techniques, along with other advanced methods like behavioral analysis and machine learning, form the backbone of next-generation anti-malware solutions, providing comprehensive protection in the ever-changing landscape of cyber threats.

Comparing Efficacy: Anti-Malware vs. Next-Generation Anti-Malware

As we've delved into the intricacies of both anti-malware and next-generation anti-malware, an essential question surfaces: how do these two compare in terms of effectiveness? To answer this question, we need to consider various dimensions, including detection capabilities, response times, and how they handle evolving threats.

Detection Capabilities

Traditional anti-malware primarily utilizes signature-based detection, which is excellent at identifying known threats. Once a piece of malware has been identified and its signature catalogued, traditional anti-malware can detect and handle it with high accuracy. However, its weakness lies in its inability to effectively handle unknown or zero-day threats – threats that have not yet been catalogued and thus do not have a known signature.

Next-generation anti-malware, on the other hand, excels in this area. By incorporating heuristic and behavioral detection techniques, alongside artificial intelligence and machine learning, next-generation anti-malware can identify new and evolving threats that do not yet have known signatures. In addition, these advanced techniques allow next-generation anti-malware to detect stealthy attacks that traditional anti-malware might miss, such as fileless malware or advanced persistent threats (APTs).

Response Times

When it comes to response times, next-generation anti-malware often outperforms traditional anti-malware, particularly in a SASE architecture. Traditional anti-malware requires regular updates to its signature database, which can be a slow process, particularly in large organizations with many endpoints. This delay could potentially allow new threats to infiltrate the system before the updated signatures are in place.

With next-generation anti-malware in a SASE framework, updates are virtually instantaneous. Cloud-based threat intelligence is continuously updated with the latest threat data, allowing next-generation anti-malware to respond to new threats as soon as they're identified. This minimizes the window of opportunity for new malware to penetrate your system.

Handling Evolving Threats

Finally, the ability to handle evolving threats is where next-generation anti-malware truly shines. Traditional anti-malware, while reliable against known threats, can struggle to adapt to the rapidly changing threat landscape. With cybercriminals constantly developing new techniques and strategies to bypass defenses, an anti-malware solution that relies solely on known signatures can quickly become outmoded.

In contrast, next-generation anti-malware is designed to evolve with the threat landscape. Its use of AI and machine learning allows it to learn from each new threat it encounters, improving its detection capabilities over time. This ability to learn and adapt makes next-generation anti-malware a formidable tool in the fight against cyber threats, offering robust protection in a world where threats are constantly evolving.

In conclusion, while traditional anti-malware still plays a crucial role in cybersecurity, next-generation anti-malware offers several advantages in terms of detection capabilities, response times, and adaptability to evolving threats. Thus, integrating next-generation anti-malware into a SASE architecture can provide comprehensive, future-proof protection against both known and unknown threats.

Chapter 11: More Firewalls?

Securing the internet

Let's begin our exploration of cloud-hosted Internet firewalls, or Firewall as a Service (FwaaS), in the context of a Secure Access Service Edge (SASE) architecture. With the rise of digital transformations and cloud migrations, traditional network perimeters have become increasingly porous and difficult to secure. FwaaS represents a new approach to network security that aligns with the distributed, cloud-first nature of modern networks.

In essence, FwaaS provides the functionality of a traditional network firewall but delivered as a cloud-based service. It inspects network traffic, screens out cyber threats, and enforces security policies, just like a traditional firewall. However, by shifting these functionalities to the cloud, FwaaS offers several key advantages that make it particularly well-suited to a SASE architecture.

One of these advantages is scalability. In a traditional network setup, scaling up your firewall capabilities usually means buying and installing more hardware. This process can be time-consuming, costly, and disruptive. With FwaaS, scaling is as simple as adjusting your service subscription. The cloud-based nature of the service means it can effortlessly adapt to accommodate changes in your network traffic, whether it's an increase in the number of remote workers or a new branch office opening.

Another advantage of FwaaS in a SASE context is the improved visibility and control it offers. In traditional networks, maintaining visibility can be a challenge, especially as networks become more distributed. Each network segment may have its own firewall with its own set of logs, making it difficult to gain a centralized view of network activity. FwaaS addresses this issue by providing a unified, cloud-based platform for managing network security. This gives you a centralized view of your entire network, making it easier to spot trends, identify threats, and enforce consistent security policies across all network segments.

FwaaS also ties in neatly with the SASE principle of integrating network and security services. In a traditional network, your firewall might be one of several standalone security appliances, each with its own management console and policy framework. This fragmentation can make security management complex and time-consuming. In contrast, FwaaS can be seamlessly integrated with other SASE services, creating a unified security platform that simplifies management and ensures consistent security enforcement.

The final advantage of FwaaS I'll touch on is cost. Traditional firewalls involve significant capital expenditure, not to mention the ongoing costs of maintenance and upgrades. FwaaS, on the other hand, operates on a subscription-based model, shifting these costs from CapEx to OpEx. This not only makes firewall services more affordable but also allows you to align your security spending with your actual needs, rather than over-provisioning to accommodate potential future growth.

In short, FwaaS represents a significant step forward in network security. It takes the robust protection offered by traditional firewalls and enhances it with the flexibility, scalability, and simplicity of a cloud-based service, making it an ideal component of a SASE architecture.

Before we continue our discussion on FwaaS and its role in SASE architecture, let's pause to take a historical look at the evolution of firewalls. This history will help us understand how firewalls have adapted over the years to keep pace with the changing landscape of networking and cybersecurity, ultimately leading to the development of FwaaS.

Packet Filtering Firewalls (Late 1980s - Early 1990s):

This is the earliest type of firewall, primarily concerned with inspecting packets of data as they pass through. They would examine the source and destination IP addresses, ports, and protocols and make a decision on whether to let the packet through based on pre-defined rules. However, these firewalls were relatively easy to bypass as they had no understanding of the data being transported.

Stateful Firewalls (Mid-1990s):

The next evolution of firewalls was stateful firewalls. These offered more advanced inspection capabilities than their packet-filtering predecessors. They maintained a state table that tracked the context of each network connection, including IP addresses, ports, and the sequence number of packets. This allowed them to prevent certain types of attacks, such as those that attempted to exploit TCP's three-way handshake.

Application-Level Gateways (Late 1990s - Early 2000s):

Also known as proxy firewalls, these operate at the application layer of the OSI model. They acted as an intermediary, creating two connections for every request - one between the client and the proxy and another between the proxy and the server. This allowed them to inspect and filter data at a much deeper level than stateful firewalls, but they were resource-intensive and could impact network performance.

Next-Generation Firewalls (NGFWs, Mid 2000s - Present):

Next-generation firewalls took the capabilities of stateful firewalls and application-level gateways and combined them into a single solution. They also added several new features, including deep packet inspection (DPI), intrusion prevention systems (IPS), and application awareness. This provided even more thorough inspection and filtering of network traffic, but the complexity and cost of managing these firewalls began to rise.

Firewall as a Service (FwaaS, Late 2010s - Present):

FwaaS represents the latest evolution of firewalls. By moving firewall functionality to the cloud, FwaaS offers the advanced security features of NGFWs but with the scalability, simplicity, and cost-effectiveness of a cloud service. This makes it ideally suited to the distributed, dynamic nature of modern networks, as encapsulated by the SASE architecture.

In the next section, we'll explore in more detail how FwaaS integrates with other SASE components and the benefits this integration brings.

FWaaS and SASE?

As we've established, FwaaS and SASE are natural bedfellows in the modern era of networking and security. However, to appreciate the full value of this union, it's vital to understand the synergy between FwaaS and other components within the SASE architecture.

A primary element of the SASE architecture that beautifully complements FwaaS is the Secure Web Gateway (SWG). With SWG responsible for implementing web filtering policies and scrutinizing web traffic for threats, pairing it with FwaaS allows for comprehensive inbound and outbound security coverage. This dual-layered approach reduces the odds of threats sneaking through unnoticed, making for a more secure network environment.

Moreover, when FwaaS is integrated with Zero Trust Network Access (ZTNA) - another core tenet of SASE -

the outcome is a highly granular access control system. With FwaaS performing broad network security functions and ZTNA focusing on individual device and user access, the risk of unauthorized access and lateral movement within the network is significantly reduced.

Furthermore, by running FwaaS in the same cloud-native environment as other SASE components such as Data Loss Prevention (DLP) and Cloud Access Security Brokers (CASB), organizations can ensure seamless interoperability and centralized policy management. In this case, if FwaaS detects suspicious behavior or a potential data breach, it can work in tandem with DLP and CASB solutions to swiftly mitigate the threat and prevent data exfiltration.

The beauty of SASE is that all these security services – FwaaS, SWG, ZTNA, DLP, and CASB, among others – are tightly interwoven within the same architecture. This integration eliminates the need for disjointed, standalone security solutions, reducing complexity and allowing for streamlined security operations.

Beyond interoperability, FwaaS within SASE brings the added advantage of improved performance. Given SASE's edge computing principles, security services are delivered as close to the user as possible, minimizing latency. As a result, FwaaS doesn't become a bottleneck in the network but instead facilitates speedy and secure connectivity.

In the SASE model, firewall services aren't just transported to the cloud; they're transformed by it. FwaaS is constructed on a cloud-native, multi-tenant architecture that allows for high scalability and adaptability. Unlike traditional firewall appliances that are rigid and restricted by their hardware limitations, FwaaS instances can be instantiated and scaled up or down on-demand. This elasticity makes it an excellent fit for organizations experiencing rapid growth or seasonal demand fluctuations.

An important feature of FwaaS in a SASE context is its ability to support both north-south and east-west inspection. North-south inspection involves examining traffic flowing in and out of the network, a task that traditional firewalls are adept at. However, with the rise of cloud and virtualization technologies, east-west traffic, that is, the traffic moving laterally within a network, has grown exponentially. This inter-VM or inter-container traffic can often bypass traditional perimeter defenses, creating a blind spot that attackers can exploit. FwaaS can ensure that this internal traffic is inspected and secured, closing the door on a potential avenue for attacks.

Moreover, FwaaS in SASE environments can be deployed in a variety of settings. Whether you have a small team working remotely, a large corporate office, or a complex multi-cloud setup, FwaaS can seamlessly adapt to your needs. It's as easy as deploying a client on the endpoint devices for remote workers or implementing a virtual appliance for larger office networks. This versatility ensures that organizations of all sizes and types can benefit from FwaaS without having to worry about compatibility or deployment issues.

One of the beauties of FwaaS is its integration with Software-Defined Wide Area Networking (SD-WAN). In the SASE architecture, SD-WAN and security functionalities coalesce, allowing for optimized and secure connectivity. With FwaaS and SD-WAN working hand in hand, organizations can ensure that they not only have a high-performing network but also one that's fortified against threats. SD-WAN technologies can optimize traffic routing, making sure that critical applications have the bandwidth they need. In contrast, FwaaS can scrutinize this traffic to prevent malicious entities from infiltrating the network. Together, they offer a balanced approach to networking – one that doesn't sacrifice security for performance or vice versa. In the following section, we'll explore a real-world use case, detailing how FwaaS in a SASE architecture can transform an organization's network security posture.

Let's consider a growing multinational corporation, CorpX, that decided to shift towards a cloud-first IT strategy, embracing SaaS solutions, and enabling a flexible work-from-anywhere policy. They found their traditional, appliance-based firewall solutions insufficient to manage this new network landscape with remote employees, cloud services, and global offices. CorpX decided to implement FwaaS as part of their SASE strategy.

The first step in their FwaaS deployment involved a comprehensive audit of their existing network security infrastructure and policies. They examined their current firewalls' capabilities, identified gaps, and defined the security features they wanted in their new FwaaS solution. This included capabilities such as deep packet inspection, intrusion prevention, application control, and web filtering.

Next, CorpX set about choosing a SASE provider that offered FwaaS as part of their suite of services. They prioritized providers that demonstrated cloud-native design, high scalability, robust security features, and excellent performance levels. After a thorough evaluation process, they selected a provider that met their requirements and showcased a clear roadmap for future enhancements.

With the SASE provider chosen, CorpX moved onto the implementation phase. They rolled out the FwaaS solution in stages, starting with their main office before extending it to their branch offices and remote workers. This gradual rollout allowed them to troubleshoot issues and adjust configurations as necessary without impacting the entire network.

The results were immediate and significant. With FwaaS in place, CorpX achieved superior visibility into their network activity, thanks to the centralized management console provided by the SASE solution. They could see all network traffic, irrespective of where it originated or where it was headed, and apply consistent policies across the entire network.

Threat detection and response times improved dramatically. FwaaS's advanced security features, combined with other SASE components like SWG and ZTNA, provided multi-layered security that swiftly identified and neutralized threats. Moreover, FwaaS's cloud-native design meant that updates and patches could be rolled out network-wide in near real-time, keeping the security features up-to-date against the latest threats.

The transformation was not just limited to security. The unified, cloud-native nature of the SASE architecture meant that CorpX saw benefits in network performance and management as well. The integration of FwaaS with SD-WAN ensured optimal network performance, and the centralization of network services resulted in simplified management and lower total cost of ownership.

In conclusion, CorpX's journey underscores the transformative impact of incorporating FwaaS into a SASE architecture. It serves as a testament to how organizations can fortify their security posture, improve network performance, and streamline management, all while supporting modern business practices like remote work and cloud adoption.

What about WAN firewalls?

As we dive deeper into the world of SASE, it's time to demystify a commonly misunderstood concept: the difference between a cloud-hosted Wide Area Network (WAN) firewall and Firewall-as-a-Service (FwaaS). While they both operate within a similar realm, there are significant differences between them, particularly in how they are deployed, managed, and how they fit within the broader SASE framework.

A cloud-hosted WAN firewall, as its name suggests, is a firewall service that is hosted in the cloud rather than being installed on-premises. This cloud-hosted model offers a range of benefits, such as ease of scaling, reduced hardware costs, and simplified management. It primarily focuses on securing the Wide Area Network, which connects an organization's various geographically distributed locations.

A cloud-hosted WAN firewall typically provides a centralized management console, where security policies can be set and applied across the entire WAN. It offers functionalities like intrusion prevention, application control, and web filtering. The firewall rules can be configured to allow or block specific types of network traffic, and deep packet inspection (DPI) can be used to inspect the contents of network packets for signs of malicious activity.

However, while a cloud-hosted WAN firewall provides essential network security functions, it doesn't usually offer the comprehensive security features that a SASE architecture demands. This is where FwaaS steps in.

Firewall-as-a-Service (FwaaS), in the context of SASE, is a comprehensive, cloud-native firewall solution that is designed to secure not just the WAN, but all network traffic, regardless of its source or destination. It provides all the functionalities of a cloud-hosted WAN firewall and adds a host of other features such as Zero Trust Network Access (ZTNA), Secure Web Gateway (SWG), and integration with other cloud-based security services.

FwaaS is built on a multi-tenant, cloud-native architecture, which allows it to scale seamlessly with the needs of the business. It can secure network traffic from any location – be it an office, a remote worker's home, or a cloud service. Its ability to inspect and secure both inbound and outbound traffic, as well as internal (east-west) traffic, makes it a vital component in a SASE environment.

First, consider scalability and adaptability. A cloud-hosted WAN firewall, while more scalable than an on-premises solution, might still face limitations when it comes to handling massive traffic volumes or sudden spikes in demand. In contrast, FwaaS, due to its cloud-native multi-tenant architecture, can scale up or down dynamically based on the load. It can quickly adapt to business needs, whether that involves accommodating a surge in remote workers or managing the increased network traffic associated with a corporate merger or acquisition.

Another critical difference lies in the nature of traffic inspection. A cloud-hosted WAN firewall traditionally focuses on inspecting north-south traffic, i.e., the data flowing into and out of the network. However, in today's multi-cloud, hybrid environments, the volume of east-west traffic – data moving laterally within the network – has grown significantly. This traffic is often internal to a virtual private cloud (VPC) or occurs between containers in a microservices architecture. FwaaS shines in this regard, providing robust inspection and security for east-west traffic, effectively mitigating the risk of lateral movement by attackers within the network.

Integration is another point of differentiation. A cloud-hosted WAN firewall may integrate with other network security tools, but this is often achieved through APIs and may not offer seamless interoperability. FwaaS, on the other hand, is inherently designed to work in conjunction with other SASE components. It can natively integrate with ZTNA, CASB, SWG, and other cloud-based security services, providing a unified, holistic security posture that is easier to manage and more resilient against threats.

Lastly, we must consider the evolution of the network perimeter. The traditional network perimeter has dissolved with the rise of remote work, BYOD policies, and cloud computing. A cloud-hosted WAN firewall, while more flexible than its on-premises counterpart, is still tied to the concept of a defined network perimeter. In contrast, FwaaS aligns with the concept of a perimeter-less, identity- and context-based network security model. It can secure access at the edge – be it a remote worker at a coffee shop, a contractor in a different country, or an IoT device on a factory floor.

While the technical differences between a cloud-hosted WAN firewall and FwaaS are fundamental, understanding the operational differences can shed light on the different use-cases for these two technologies.

The operational model of a cloud-hosted WAN firewall revolves around protecting the perimeter of a geographically distributed WAN. The cloud-hosted element simplifies the management and reduces the overhead of maintaining physical hardware across multiple locations. This can be quite beneficial for organizations with multiple remote locations but with a network traffic pattern that's mostly centralized.

On the other hand, FwaaS operates on a broader scale. It goes beyond just the WAN perimeter and provides security for all network traffic, regardless of the source or destination. This holistic approach to network security aligns perfectly with the evolving work patterns where users, devices, applications, and data are located everywhere.

In terms of management and configuration, FwaaS generally offers a unified management console from which all the network security policies can be defined and enforced. This includes firewall rules, ZTNA policies, SWG configurations, and more. This centralization dramatically simplifies the task of managing network security, particularly for businesses with a diverse network landscape that includes remote workers, multiple offices, and cloud services.

In contrast, while a cloud-hosted WAN firewall also provides centralized management, it might not have the same level of seamless integration with other network security tools. You may need to configure and manage each tool separately, which can add to the complexity and overhead.

Finally, let's consider cost. While a cloud-hosted WAN firewall may offer cost benefits over a traditional on-premises firewall, it may still involve separate costs for each component of your network security stack. FwaaS, as part of a SASE framework, is often subscription-based, bundling numerous security functions into a single, per-user cost. This can lead to significant cost savings and also offers more predictable expenditure over time.

Now that we understand the operational differences, let's explore how to choose between a cloud-hosted WAN firewall and FwaaS.

Why keep the WAN and Internet Firewall separate?

As we dig deeper into the discussion about firewalls within the SASE context, we find that the differentiation between Internet and WAN firewalls, or more specifically, Firewall-as-a-Service (FwaaS) and cloud-hosted WAN firewalls, is not just a mere matter of semantics. Understanding why it's crucial to maintain a clear separation between these two types of firewalls can significantly influence how we approach and build our network security architecture.

To begin with, let's unravel the fundamental differences between Internet and WAN firewalls.

1. Scope of Protection: An Internet firewall is generally responsible for protecting an organization's network from threats originating from the Internet. It scrutinizes all traffic entering and exiting the network, blocking any malicious or unauthorized packets. Conversely, a WAN firewall primarily secures the Wide Area Network, including all branch offices and data centers, against internal and external threats.

2. Placement in the Network: Internet firewalls are typically deployed at the network's edge, where the network interfaces with the Internet, creating a buffer zone between the internal network and the rest of

the world. In contrast, WAN firewalls are often placed between different parts of the organization's WAN, such as between branch offices or between a branch office and the data center.

3. Focus of Security: While Internet firewalls are mainly concerned with inbound and outbound traffic (north-south traffic), WAN firewalls also focus on securing traffic moving laterally within the network (east-west traffic). This is particularly crucial in today's complex and distributed network environments, where threats often move laterally within the network.

Given these differences, it's clear that Internet firewalls and WAN firewalls play distinct roles in a network security architecture. But why is it important to keep these two types of firewalls separate?

To answer this question, let's look at the unique advantages and roles of FwaaS and cloud-hosted WAN firewalls in a SASE context.

FwaaS, being a comprehensive, cloud-native security solution, provides robust protection against Internet threats. As it sits at the edge of the network, it inspects and secures all traffic entering and exiting the network, thereby shielding the entire network ecosystem from any external threats.

FwaaS, in the context of SASE, also extends its capabilities to support other cloud-based security services such as Secure Web Gateway (SWG), Zero Trust Network Access (ZTNA), and more. This integrated approach to network security allows FwaaS to provide a consistent security posture across all network traffic, regardless of its source or destination. By maintaining FwaaS as a distinct entity in the SASE framework, you can harness its full potential and ensure a comprehensive, unified network security.

On the other hand, a cloud-hosted WAN firewall plays a crucial role in securing the organization's Wide Area Network. By being strategically placed within the WAN, it provides a crucial layer of protection against threats that may emerge from within the network. This is especially important given the increasing prevalence of insider threats and lateral movement by attackers within the network.

A cloud-hosted WAN firewall also offers benefits such as centralized management, ease of scalability, and reduced hardware costs. Keeping it separate from the Internet firewall allows for more focused and efficient management of WAN security. It also ensures that the unique requirements and traffic patterns of the WAN are adequately catered to.

So, while FwaaS and cloud-hosted WAN firewalls both form an integral part of a SASE framework, keeping them distinct allows each to play to its strengths, providing a robust, layered defense that secures all aspects of network traffic.

Implementing Firewall-as-a-Service (FwaaS) and cloud-hosted WAN firewalls in a Secure Access Service Edge (SASE) context is a significant undertaking that involves careful planning, consideration, and execution. Here are some key steps and considerations that can guide you on this journey.

Step 1: Understand Your Network

Before diving into the implementation, it's crucial to have a clear understanding of your existing network architecture. This includes knowing your network's size, complexity, traffic patterns, and security requirements. Understanding the distinct roles that FwaaS and WAN firewalls play in your network will also be critical in this phase.

Step 2: Define Your Security Policies

Your security policies should serve as the foundation of your SASE implementation. These policies should reflect your organization's security goals and compliance requirements. They should also take into account the specific features and capabilities of FwaaS and WAN firewalls. Keep in mind that these policies will likely need to be updated and refined over time as your network and security needs evolve.

Step 3: Choose Your SASE Provider

Choosing a SASE provider is a critical decision that can significantly impact the success of your implementation. Consider factors such as the provider's reputation, the breadth and depth of their SASE offering, their integration capabilities, and their support and service levels.

Step 4: Plan Your Deployment

Consider the deployment process for both FwaaS and WAN firewalls. This will likely involve a phased approach, starting with a small pilot deployment and gradually expanding to the rest of your network. Ensure that you have a robust plan for managing and mitigating any disruptions or issues that may arise during the deployment process.

Step 5: Monitor and Adjust

After deploying FwaaS and WAN firewalls, it's important to continually monitor their performance and effectiveness. This includes tracking key metrics, analyzing security logs, and staying alert for any new or emerging threats. Be prepared to adjust your security policies, configurations, or even your SASE provider, based on these observations.

In this chapter, we delved into the critical but nuanced distinctions between Firewall-as-a-Service (FwaaS) and cloud-hosted WAN firewalls. As we've seen, the two are complementary facets of the network security picture and both play key roles in a Secure Access Service Edge (SASE) architecture.

An Internet firewall, as represented by FwaaS in the SASE context, provides a robust shield for the organization against external threats. By operating at the edge of the network, it effectively inspects all inbound and outbound traffic, safeguarding against attacks originating from the Internet. Its integration with other cloud-based security services further extends its protective coverage, thereby delivering a unified, comprehensive security posture.

Meanwhile, the cloud-hosted WAN firewall focuses on securing the Wide Area Network, watching over the traffic flowing between different components of the WAN. Given the increasingly distributed nature of organizations, with branch offices, remote workers, and data centers often spread across multiple geographical locations, a cloud-hosted WAN firewall forms an essential layer of defense.

As such, it's crucial to understand and maintain the distinction between FwaaS and WAN firewalls. Each has unique roles and strengths that can be maximized when they are deployed separately in a SASE framework. From an operational standpoint, this can also lead to more effective and efficient management of network security.

We also discussed the process of implementing these firewalls within the SASE framework, underlining the importance of planning, choosing the right SASE provider, and continuously monitoring and adjusting your approach as needed.

In summary, while FwaaS and cloud-hosted WAN firewalls form distinct elements of your SASE architecture, they come together to provide a robust, comprehensive defense that safeguards all aspects of your network traffic, thereby enabling a secure, efficient, and scalable network ecosystem for your organization. As network demands continue to evolve, understanding and leveraging the capabilities of these tools will be essential to navigating the ever-changing landscape of network security.

Chapter 12: The Cloud Access Security Broker (CASB)

In the rapidly evolving landscape of digital connectivity, the Secure Access Service Edge (SASE) framework has emerged as a revolutionary approach to network and security architecture. As we delve into Chapter 12 of our journey through the world of SASE, we're presented with an indispensable component of this framework: the Cloud Access Security Broker, or CASB. CASB plays a pivotal role in extending the security perimeter beyond traditional boundaries, ensuring data protection and compliance as organizations embrace cloud technologies and remote workforces. In this chapter, we will unravel the intricacies of CASB, understanding its significance and the ways it bolsters the SASE paradigm.

What is a CASB?

The world of IT is filled with many different acronyms (which are often difficult to remember), so let's begin with the most obvious question: What is a CASB?

A cloud access security broker (CASB) is typically cloud-hosted software, or on-premises software/hardware, that act as a middleman between users and cloud service providers.

CASB addresses gaps in security and extends across multiple environments including software-as-a-service (SaaS), platform-as-a-service (PaaS), and infrastructure-as-a-service (IaaS) offerings. In addition to providing visibility, a CASB also allows organizations to extend the reach of their security policies from their existing on-premises infrastructure to the cloud and create new policies for cloud-specific context.

The CASB serves as a policy enforcement centre, consolidating multiple types of security policy enforcement and applying them to everything your business utilizes in the cloud — regardless of what sort of device is attempting to access it, including unmanaged smartphones, IoT devices, or personal laptops.

CASBs have become a vital part of enterprise security, allowing businesses to safely use the cloud while protecting sensitive corporate data.

Are you still confused about CASB? Let's simplify:

- Cloud = Any form of data or applications not hosted on-premises
- Access = The means of who, and what is allowed access to something.
- Security = Ensuring data remains safe

- Broker = The middleman who connects all the dots, and applies the policy.

The Role of CASB in SASE

As we've emphasized throughout our exploration of SASE, the traditional approach of securing a centralized network perimeter no longer suffices in an age of cloud adoption and remote work. With employees accessing applications and data from various locations and devices, the perimeter has become nebulous. CASB bridges this gap by acting as a guardian of the data itself, irrespective of where it resides or is accessed from.

Key Functions of CASB

1. Visibility and Discovery: One of the initial challenges in securing a sprawling digital ecosystem is gaining visibility into the shadow IT landscape. CASB solutions offer real-time insights into the applications being used, allowing organizations to identify potential security risks and compliance breaches.

2. Data Loss Prevention (DLP): Protecting sensitive data from leaks or unauthorized sharing is a critical concern. CASBs employ DLP mechanisms to monitor and control the movement of sensitive information, both

within and outside the organization's network.

3. Access Control: CASBs enforce granular access policies, ensuring that users are granted access only to the data and applications they are authorized to use. This helps prevent unauthorized access and reduces the risk of insider threats.

4. Threat Protection: As cyber threats continue to evolve, CASBs serve as a frontline defense against malicious activities. They leverage advanced threat detection mechanisms, such as behavior analytics and anomaly detection, to identify and mitigate potential threats.

5. Compliance Monitoring: Staying compliant with industry regulations and data protection laws is non-negotiable for modern businesses. CASBs assist in monitoring and ensuring compliance by providing real-time visibility into data usage and enforcing policies to meet regulatory requirements.

Let's dig in further.

Visibility

The first step is Visibility. Visibility is about understanding what is happening on your network to then make informed decisions.

Large businesses often have employees accessing many applications in multiple cloud environments, distributed across the world. When cloud usage is outside the view/control of IT, enterprise data is no longer bound by the company's governance, risk, or compliance policies. This is where things often go wrong.

To safeguard users, confidential data, (and intellectual property); a CASB solution provides comprehensive visibility into cloud app usage. This often includes user information such as device and location data.

The cloud discovery analysis provides a risk assessment for each cloud service in use. This level of visibility allows enterprise security professionals to decide whether to continue allowing access to applications or if they should block the app.

This information is also useful in helping shape and defining more granular controls. This could include granting varying levels of access to apps and data based on an individual's device, location, and job function.

Compliance

Wait, don't run away, Compliance isn't as boring as it sounds!

While businesses can outsource all of their systems and data storage to the cloud, they maintain responsibility for compliance with regulations governing the privacy and safety of enterprise data.

A CASB can help maintain compliance in the cloud by addressing a wide variety of compliance regulations such as HIPAA, as well as regulatory requirements such as ISO 27001, PCI DSS, and more.

A CASB solution can determine the areas of highest risk in terms of compliance and provide direction as to what the security team should focus on to resolve them.

Data Security

Cloud adoption has removed many of the barriers preventing effective collaboration at distance, such as a heavy uptick in working-from-home in 2020 (for no apparent reason.) However, as much as the seamless movement of data can be of benefit, it can also come at a tremendous cost for businesses with an interest in protecting sensitive and confidential information.

While on-premises data-loss protection (DLP) solutions are designed to safeguard data, their ability to do so often does not extend to cloud services and lacks cloud context.

CASB provides the ability to see when, and how, sensitive content is being transferred. Whether this is data that travels to or from the cloud, within the cloud, and cloud to cloud.

By deploying security features like access control, information rights management, encryption, and policy control, enterprise data leaks can be minimized.

Threat Protection

This is the interesting bit.
Whether through negligence or malicious intent, employees and third parties with stolen credentials can leak or steal sensitive data from cloud services.
To help pinpoint anomalous user behaviour, CASBs can compile a comprehensive view of regular usage patterns and use it as a basis for comparison. This allows a CASB solution to continuously improve the accuracy of the data output, with minimal interaction from their users.
To protect against threats coming from cloud services, a CASB can use capabilities such as adaptive access control, static and dynamic malware analysis, prioritized analysis, and threat intelligence to block malware.

Deployment Models

CASB solutions can be deployed in various ways, catering to an organization's specific needs:

1. API-Based CASBs: These solutions integrate with cloud applications through APIs (Application Programming Interfaces), allowing for real-time visibility and control over data flows. API-based CASBs are suitable for environments where direct

network traffic interception might not be feasible.

2. Proxy-Based CASBs: In this model, traffic is routed through a CASB proxy, allowing for deep inspection and control of data as it travels between users and cloud applications. Proxy-based CASBs are effective in scenarios where API integration might be limited or insufficient.

3. Forward Proxy vs. Reverse Proxy: Forward proxies are situated within an organization's network, intercepting outbound traffic. Reverse proxies, on the other hand, are deployed in the cloud, intercepting incoming traffic. Organizations might opt for one or both proxies based on their requirements.

4.

Challenges and Considerations

While CASBs offer a comprehensive solution for securing data in the cloud-centric era, there are challenges and considerations to bear in mind:

1. Complexity: Implementing and managing CASB solutions can be intricate, requiring a deep understanding of an organization's cloud applications and data flows.

2. Performance Impact: Depending on the deployment model, CASBs might introduce

latency as traffic is inspected and controlled. Balancing security with performance is crucial.

3. Integration: Ensuring seamless integration with existing security infrastructure and policies is essential to avoid disrupting established workflows.

4. User Experience: Striking a balance between enforcing security controls and maintaining a smooth user experience is vital to prevent frustration among employees.

Why do you need a CASB solution?

Good question.

Services and Software used to be primarily hosted on a Server somewhere within the Corporate WAN. However, if you've been paying attention to the shifting nature of how people are working, you may have noticed that most applications are now being moved to the Cloud. RIP Datacenters.

Maintaining both visibility and control in these environments is essential to ensure your business can continue to operate efficiently. This may include meeting compliance requirements, safeguarding your enterprise from attack, and allowing your employees to safely use cloud services without introducing additional high risk to your enterprise.

Why do you need a CASB? Simple - you need to protect your network against the Cloud, whilst also granting access to the Cloud at the same time.

Chapter 13: DLP and Me – Data Loss Prevention

In an era defined by interconnectedness and digital transformation, data has become one of the most valuable assets for businesses across industries. However, with this increasing reliance on data comes the heightened risk of data breaches, leaks, and unauthorized exposure. Enter Data Loss Prevention (DLP), a vital component of modern cybersecurity strategies that seeks to mitigate these risks and protect sensitive information. As we embark on this deep dive into the realm of DLP, we'll uncover its essential concepts, strategies, and its role in ensuring the integrity and security of data in an ever-evolving technological landscape.

Understanding Data Loss Prevention (DLP)

At its core, DLP is a set of tools, processes, and policies designed to prevent the unauthorized transmission, sharing, or exposure of sensitive data within an organization. This sensitive data can include personally identifiable information (PII), financial records, intellectual property, customer data, and more. DLP operates under the fundamental premise that prevention is the best strategy to avoid data breaches and their subsequent consequences.

Why DLP Matters in Today's World

In the digital age, where data traverses networks, cloud platforms, and devices at an unprecedented pace, the potential for data loss is a pressing concern. Data breaches not only incur significant financial costs but also damage a company's reputation and erode customer trust. DLP addresses these concerns by offering a multi-faceted approach to safeguarding sensitive information.

Key Components of DLP

- **Data Discovery:** The first step in DLP implementation involves identifying where sensitive data resides. This can be across various storage systems, servers, databases, and endpoints. DLP solutions scan and classify data, creating an inventory of sensitive information.

- **Data Classification:** Not all data is equally sensitive. DLP systems assign labels to data based on its sensitivity level. This classification helps in defining appropriate protection measures for different types of data.

- **Content Inspection:** DLP tools employ content inspection mechanisms to analyze data in transit, at rest, or in use. This involves pattern matching, keyword analysis, and even machine learning to identify sensitive content.

- **Policy Enforcement:** DLP relies on predefined policies to dictate how sensitive data should be handled. Policies can range from preventing certain types of data from leaving the organization to alerting administrators when data access or sharing violates established rules.

- **Encryption and Tokenization:** To enhance security, DLP solutions can employ encryption or tokenization techniques. Encryption ensures that even if data is intercepted, it remains unreadable without the decryption key. Tokenization replaces sensitive data with surrogate values, maintaining the format while keeping the actual content secure.

- **Monitoring and Incident Response:** DLP solutions continuously monitor data flow and user behavior. When policy violations are detected, alerts are generated, and actions are taken to mitigate risks. Incident response capabilities allow organizations to react swiftly to breaches or potential leaks.

Strategies for Effective DLP Implementation

- **Comprehensive Policy Design:** Crafting well-defined policies is the cornerstone of successful DLP. Policies should cover both inbound and outbound data traffic and account for various scenarios, such as email attachments, cloud storage, and data transfers.
- **User Education and Awareness:** Employees play a significant role in data protection. Conducting training sessions to educate users about data handling best practices and the importance of DLP can greatly reduce the risk of accidental data exposure.

- **Collaboration with Legal and Compliance Teams:** DLP policies should align with industry regulations and legal requirements. Collaboration with legal and compliance teams ensures that data protection measures adhere to the necessary standards.
- **Continuous Monitoring and Refinement:** Cyber threats and data usage patterns evolve over time. Regularly monitoring and refining DLP policies and configurations keep them effective and adaptable to changing circumstances.

DLP in the Context of SASE

As we've explored in previous chapters of our SASE journey, the Secure Access Service Edge framework seeks to address the challenges posed by cloud adoption and remote work. DLP plays an integral role in this context by extending data protection to remote users and cloud applications. By integrating DLP mechanisms into the SASE architecture, organizations ensure that data security remains robust regardless of the user's location or the data's storage medium.

Challenges and Considerations

While DLP holds tremendous potential in enhancing data security, there are challenges to overcome during implementation:

- **False Positives and Negatives:** Striking the right balance between thorough content inspection and avoiding false positives (flagging benign actions as violations) or false negatives (failing to detect actual breaches) can be challenging.
- **Sensitive Data Classification:** Accurate data classification is essential for effective DLP. Misclassification can lead to data exposure or unnecessary restrictions.
- **Performance Impact:** Introducing DLP mechanisms, such as content inspection, can impact network and application performance. Finding the equilibrium between security and performance is crucial.
- **User Privacy Concerns:** While DLP is aimed at safeguarding data, it must be implemented in a way that respects user privacy and doesn't infringe on personal communication.

In the age of digital interconnectedness, data has become both a powerful asset and a potential liability. Data Loss Prevention (DLP) emerges as a critical shield against the risk of data breaches, leaks, and unauthorized exposure. Its multifaceted approach, encompassing data discovery, classification, content inspection, and policy enforcement, ensures that sensitive information remains secure across the vast digital landscape.

In our ongoing exploration of the Secure Access Service Edge framework, DLP holds a pivotal role in extending data protection beyond the traditional boundaries of the network. As organizations adapt to cloud technologies and remote work, DLP's importance in the broader context of SASE becomes increasingly evident. However, as we navigate the complexities of DLP implementation, it's important to strike a balance between robust data protection and the need for seamless workflows. The challenges posed by false positives, performance impact, and user privacy concerns must be addressed conscientiously.

As we conclude our dive into the realm of Data Loss Prevention, it's clear that DLP is not just a technology but a strategic imperative for modern businesses. By safeguarding sensitive information, organizations fortify their reputation, build trust, and ensure compliance with regulatory standards. In an era where data is the lifeblood of innovation, DLP stands as a sentinel, guarding against threats and enabling the secure progression of the digital age.

Chapter 14: Single Vendor, or Multi-Vendor SASE?

In this chapter, our exploration of the intricate tapestry of Secure Access Service Edge (SASE) brings us to a decisive crossroads. Here, organizations embarking on the transformative journey of secure digital transformation face a momentous choice: the adoption of a single-vendor or a multi-vendor approach to weaving the fabric of SASE. As we delve into the depths of this critical decision, the intricate interplay between these two divergent paths unfolds, offering a profound insight into the nuances, challenges, and opportunities that define the selection of the right SASE vendor strategy.

The Tale of Single-Vendor SASE: Unity Amidst Complexity

Within the realm of SASE, the single-vendor approach emerges as a testament to the power of unity. Organizations embracing this path opt to forge their SASE architecture by entrusting all its components - from the foundations of networking to the guardians of security and management - to the dominion of a solitary vendor. The allure here is not merely the promise of a seamlessly interwoven array of components, but the prospect of a harmonious symphony that reverberates through the corridors of integration, support, and centralized management.

In this realm of unity, the advantages of the single-vendor approach reveal themselves in full grandeur. Imagine an orchestra directed by a single conductor, each instrument playing in perfect harmony to create a symphony of unified vision. In a similar vein, a unified SASE solution orchestrated by a single vendor offers an interface through which configurations, monitoring, and maintenance are conducted in a seamless choreography. Integration, the cornerstone of this approach, is not an arduous puzzle to solve but an elegant dance of components that naturally fit together, reducing compatibility concerns and accelerating the march toward deployment.

However, as the single-vendor symphony plays its melodious tune, it casts shadows that warrant consideration. While unity beckons, there exists the specter of vendor lock-in, a potential dependency on a sole vendor that could complicate future strategic pivots. Furthermore, the harmonious path of integration might necessitate sacrifices in the realm of specialized best-of-breed solutions, as the allure of seamless cohesion may lead to a relinquishing of certain bespoke elements that other vendors might offer. As the narrative of single-vendor SASE unfolds, the tension between unity and potential constraints becomes a thread woven into its very fabric.

The Odyssey of Multi-Vendor SASE: Crafting Diversity Amidst Choice

On the flip side of the coin, the multi-vendor approach to SASE presents a realm of diversity and choice. Within this landscape, organizations have the liberty to curate their SASE architecture by selecting the finest offerings from a constellation of vendors, tailoring a solution that aligns exquisitely with their specific needs.

In this realm of choice, the virtues of the multi-vendor approach shine with a resplendent brilliance. It is akin to a bazaar where vendors offer an array of treasures, each beckoning with distinct advantages. The beauty lies in the possibility to select solutions that best resonate with the organization's aspirations. This approach not only quenches the thirst for innovation but also affords the freedom to escape the chains of vendor lock-in. A symphony composed of components from different vendors allows for agile shifts and realignments as the organization's journey evolves, like a ship navigating its course with the wind of flexibility billowing its sails.

Yet, the journey through the realm of diversity is not without its trials. The tapestry of multi-vendor SASE, while rich and intricate, requires the skilful weaving of threads that originate from disparate sources.

Integration, the harmonious dance of components, transforms into a symphony of coordination, where each note must be precisely timed to create a unified composition. The management of multiple vendors and their solutions, akin to a conductor orchestrating an ensemble, demands finesse and attention to ensure the harmonious performance of the SASE symphony.

The Crossroads: A Confluence of Considerations

Amidst the sprawling expanse of single-vendor and multi-vendor SASE landscapes, the decision to tread one path or the other is not a binary choice, but rather a multidimensional contemplation that is entwined with an organization's essence, objectives, and technological fabric.

The path chosen, whether unified or diversified, resonates deeply with an organization's core. It is an exploration of the soulful objectives that define the strategic voyage, a journey that aligns with the current landscape of infrastructure while embracing the future horizons of growth. It is a narrative that acknowledges the strength of existing vendor relationships, the potential for partnerships, and the orchestration of compliance and security that form the armour protecting the organization's digital realm.

The Overture's Grand Finale

As the curtain falls on this chapter, the dichotomy of single-vendor and multi-vendor SASE paths stands as a testament to the dynamic interplay between unity and diversity. The decision made at this crossroads shapes the foundation of an organization's SASE implementation, defining the contours of its digital transformation odyssey. In a world where the tides of technology are ceaseless and the winds of change unforgiving, the choice forged now propels the organization toward a future defined by secure digital connectivity and strategic resilience.

In short, whether you adopt a single or multi-vendor approach to SASE, the concepts remain the same. You need to ensure all edges are connected, secured, and protected. If you do not, then things will break, and your life will be unhappy.
My recommendation? Use a single-vendor whenever possible. Yes, I had fun writing this chapter. How could you guess?

Chapter 15: So, Am I a SASE Expert Yet?

As we reach the culmination of our journey through the intricacies of SASE, you might find yourself reflecting on the wealth of knowledge and insights gained. From the foundational concepts to the nuanced intricacies, you have navigated the labyrinthine landscape of SASE, grasping the essence of its transformative power. But the question that echoes in your mind is, "So, am I a SASE expert yet?"

Becoming a true expert in the realm of SASE is not a destination but a continuous journey. It's a journey marked not only by the accumulation of knowledge but also by the practical application of that knowledge in the ever-evolving world of technology and security. Your expertise, like a fine-tuned instrument, will resonate through your decisions, strategies, and actions as you steer your organization toward the shores of secure digital transformation.

The Signposts of Expertise

- **Comprehensive Understanding:** Expertise in SASE is rooted in a deep understanding of the framework's core components, its significance in the evolving digital landscape, and its potential to reshape the way organizations approach networking and security.

- **Holistic Viewpoint:** As a SASE expert, you possess the ability to see beyond isolated components and understand the interconnectedness of networking, security, and cloud services within the SASE architecture.

- **Adaptability:** The realm of cybersecurity is in perpetual motion. An expert in SASE is one who can adapt to the changing threat landscape, adopting new tools and strategies to safeguard against emerging risks.

- **Strategic Vision**: Your expertise empowers you to not only react to threats but also to proactively architect secure solutions that align with your organization's goals and growth trajectory.

- **Problem-Solving**: Whether it is mitigating a security breach, optimizing network performance, or ensuring compliance, your expertise enables you to approach challenges with a systematic problem-solving mindset.

The Expert's Role in the Journey

Becoming a SASE expert signifies more than mastering terminology and concepts. It is about being a catalyst for change within your organization. As you guide the implementation of SASE, you will be at the forefront of reshaping the network and security landscape, fortifying your organization's digital perimeter against emerging threats.

Your expertise will empower you to bridge gaps between technical teams, security professionals, and business stakeholders. It will enable you to communicate the value of SASE, align its deployment with strategic objectives, and champion a culture of security awareness across the organization.

Embracing the Continuous Journey

The realm of SASE is in perpetual motion, as is the journey of expertise. Innovative technologies will emerge, threat vectors will evolve, and the demands of the digital landscape will continue to shift. Your role as a SASE expert is not to rest on your laurels but to embrace the ongoing learning process, stay curious, and adapt to the changing tides of the industry.

As you reflect on the chapters you have journeyed through, remember that expertise is not a destination; it is a voyage. Your knowledge is your compass, your experience is your map, and your determination is your vessel. Each day presents an opportunity to expand your expertise, refine your skills, and contribute to the ever-evolving story of SASE.

So, are you a SASE expert yet? Yes, you have come a long way, grasping the essence of SASE's transformative potential. But remember, the journey is never truly over. As you step forward, embrace the challenges, and continue to explore the ever-expanding horizons of Secure Access Service Edge, you are not just a SASE expert—you are an architect of secure digital futures.

Until next time, you stay SASE.

Appendix: SASE Glossary

Acronym	Meaning	Brief Explanation
SASE	Secure Access Service Edge	A comprehensive framework that combines networking and security services in a cloud-based architecture.
CASB	Cloud Access Security Broker	A security solution that ensures data protection and compliance for cloud applications.
DLP	Data Loss Prevention	A set of tools and processes that prevent unauthorized transmission, sharing, or exposure of sensitive data.
PII	Personally Identifiable Information	Information that can be used to identify an

		individual, such as name, email, address, or social security number.
API	Application Programming Interface	A set of rules that allow different software applications to communicate with each other.
VPN	Virtual Private Network	A secure, encrypted connection that enables remote users to access a private network over the internet.
SD-WAN	Software-Defined Wide Area Network	A technology that enables efficient and secure communication between different locations over a wide area network.
ZTNA	Zero Trust Network Access	A security model that treats all users and devices as potential threats and requires continuous

		verification for access.
WAN	Wide Area Network	A network that spans a larger geographical area, connecting multiple smaller networks such as local area networks (LANs).
Cloud	Cloud Computing	The delivery of computing services (such as storage, processing power, and applications) over the internet, often referred to as "the cloud."
Endpoint	Endpoint Device	A device, such as a computer, smartphone, or tablet, that serves as an entry point for communication between users and networks.
Proxy	Proxy Server	A server that acts as an intermediary between users and the internet,

		forwarding requests and responses to enhance security and privacy.
Firewall	Firewall	A security device or software that monitors and controls incoming and outgoing network traffic based on predefined security rules.
Compliance	Regulatory Compliance	The adherence to laws, regulations, and industry standards pertaining to data security, privacy, and ethical practices.
Anomaly Detection	Anomaly Detection	A technique used to identify patterns or behaviors that deviate from the norm, often indicating potential security threats or

		irregularities.
API Gateway	Application Programming Interface Gateway	A server that acts as an API proxy, enabling the management, authentication, and routing of API requests between clients and backend services.
NAT	Network Address Translation	A technique that modifies network address information in data packets, allowing multiple devices to share a single public IP address.
IoT	Internet of Things	A network of interconnected physical devices (such as smart appliances and sensors) that can collect and exchange data over the internet.
PaaS	Platform as a Service	A cloud computing service that

		provides a platform allowing developers to build, deploy, and manage applications without managing the underlying infrastructure.
IaaS	Infrastructure as a Service	A cloud computing service that offers virtualized computing resources over the internet, including storage, networking, and virtual machines.
DMZ	Demilitarized Zone	A network segment that acts as a buffer zone between an internal network and the internet, often containing public-facing servers.
Edge	Edge Computing	A computing model that processes data closer to the source

		of data generation (edge devices), reducing latency and improving real-time analysis.
MPLS	Multiprotocol Label Switching	A routing technique used in telecommunications networks to direct data packets along predetermined paths, increasing efficiency and reducing congestion.
BYOD	Bring Your Own Device	A policy that allows employees to use their personal devices (such as laptops, smartphones, or tablets) for work purposes.
API	Application Programming Interface	A set of protocols and tools that enables different software applications to communicate and

		interact with each other.
NAC	Network Access Control	A security technology that enforces policies to control access to network resources based on a user's identity and device health.
SaaS	Software as a Service	A cloud computing service that delivers software applications over the internet on a subscription basis.
MFA	Multi-Factor Authentication	A security mechanism that requires users to provide two or more forms of identification before gaining access to a system or application.
DNS	Domain Name System	A system that translates human-friendly domain names into IP

		addresses, enabling users to access websites using recognizable names.
SIEM	Security Information and Event Management	A software solution that provides real-time analysis of security alerts generated by various hardware and software infrastructure.
RADIUS	Remote Authentication Dial-In User Service	A networking protocol that provides centralized authentication, authorization, and accounting management for users connecting to networks.
MDM	Mobile Device Management	A solution for managing and securing mobile devices, such as smartphones and tablets, in an

		organization.
API Gateway	Application Programming Interface Gateway	A server that acts as an API proxy, enabling the management,
IPS	Intrusion Prevention System	A security solution that monitors network traffic for malicious activity and takes actions to prevent unauthorized access or attacks.
AM	Access Management	A set of processes and technologies used to manage and control user access to resources within an organization's network.
NGFW	Next-Generation Firewall	An advanced firewall that combines traditional firewall functionality with additional security features, such as application control

		and intrusion prevention.
APT	Advanced Persistent Threat	A targeted and sophisticated cyberattack that involves prolonged and stealthy access to a network to steal sensitive information.
WAF	Web Application Firewall	A security solution that protects web applications from various online threats, such as SQL injection and cross-site scripting attacks.
EDR	Endpoint Detection and Response	A cybersecurity solution that monitors endpoint devices for signs of malicious activities and provides real-time incident response capabilities.
IDS	Intrusion Detection System	A security system that detects

		unauthorized access or suspicious activities by analyzing network traffic or host-based logs.
SIEM	Security Information and Event Management	A software solution that provides real-time analysis of security alerts generated by various hardware and software infrastructure.
UTM	Unified Threat Management	A comprehensive security solution that combines multiple security features, such as firewall, antivirus, and intrusion detection, into a single platform.
ATP	Advanced Threat Protection	A suite of security solutions designed to detect, analyze, and respond to advanced and sophisticated cyber

		threats that bypass traditional security mechanisms.
SOC	Security Operations Center	A centralized unit within an organization responsible for monitoring, detecting, analyzing, and responding to cybersecurity incidents.
SOAR	Security Orchestration, Automation, and Response	A solution that combines security orchestration and automation to streamline and accelerate incident response processes.
PKI	Public Key Infrastructure	A system of hardware, software, policies, and standards that manages digital keys and certificates for secure communications

		and authentication.
VPN	Virtual Private Network	A secure, encrypted connection that enables remote users to access a private network over the internet.
BYOD	Bring Your Own Device	A policy that allows employees to use their personal devices (such as laptops, smartphones, or tablets) for work purposes.
MFA	Multi-Factor Authentication	A security mechanism that requires users to provide two or more forms of identification before gaining access to a system or application.
DNS	Domain Name System	A system that translates human-friendly domain names into IP addresses, enabling

		users to access websites using recognizable names.
RADIUS	Remote Authentication Dial-In User Service	A networking protocol that provides centralized authentication, authorization, and accounting management for users connecting to networks.
MDM	Mobile Device Management	A solution for managing and securing mobile devices, such as smartphones and tablets, in an organization.
IPSec	Internet Protocol Security	A suite of protocols used to secure internet communications by authenticating and encrypting each packet of data.
SSL/TLS	Secure Sockets	Protocols that

	Layer / Transport Layer Security	provide secure, encrypted communication over the internet, often used to secure data transmission between web browsers and servers.
SAML	Security Assertion Markup Language	An XML-based standard for exchanging authentication and authorization data between parties, commonly used in single sign-on (SSO) scenarios.
OAuth	Open Authorization	An authorization protocol that allows applications to securely access resources on behalf of a user, without exposing the user's credentials.
RBAC	Role-Based Access Control	A security approach that assigns permissions

		and access rights based on users' roles and responsibilities within an organization.
VDI	Virtual Desktop Infrastructure	A technology that virtualizes desktop environments, allowing users to access their desktops and applications remotely from various devices.
SSL VPN	Secure Sockets Layer Virtual Private Network	A VPN technology that provides secure remote access to internal network resources using SSL/TLS encryption, without the need for client software.
NAT	Network Address Translation	A technique that modifies network address information in data packets, allowing

		multiple devices to share a single public IP address.
NIDS	Network-based Intrusion Detection System	A security system that detects unauthorized access or suspicious activities by analyzing network traffic or host-based logs.
HIDS	Host-based Intrusion Detection System	A security system that monitors activities on individual computers or hosts for signs of malicious activities or security breaches.
HIPS	Host-based Intrusion Prevention System	A security system that monitors and prevents unauthorized activities or attacks on individual computers or hosts.
AAV	Advanced	A next-generation

	Antivirus	antivirus solution that uses machine learning and behavior analysis to detect and prevent new and unknown threats.
PAM	Privileged Access Management	A solution that controls and monitors privileged access to critical systems and data, reducing the risk of insider threats and unauthorized access.

Printed in Great Britain
by Amazon

40561186R00099